FAST P⏰LYMER CLAY

Speedy techniques and projects for crafters in a hurry

SUE HEASER

NORTH LIGHT BOOKS
Cincinnati, Ohio

First published in North America by
North Light Books
an imprint of F&W Publications. Inc.
4700 East Galbraith Rd
Cincinnati
Ohio
OH 45236
USA
Tel: 1-800-289-0963

First published in Great Britain in 2003
by Collins & Brown Limited
The Chrysalis Building
Bramley Road
London W10 6SP

A member of **Chrysalis** Books plc

1 3 5 7 9 8 6 4 2

British Library Cataloguing-in-Publication Data:
A catalogue record for this book is available from
the British Library.

ISBN 1-58180-450-4

Photography by Colin Bowling
Designed by Malcolm Couch
Project managed by Emma Baxter
Copy-edited by Fiona Corbridge

Reproduction by Classicscan, Singapore
Printed and bound by Times Offset (M) Sdn Bhd, Malaysia

Contents

Introduction

Polymer clay, or oven-baked modeling clay, is an exciting new art material for the twenty-first century. For many years, polymer clay was largely a children's toy, before increasing numbers of artists and crafters realized its wonderful potential, and began to push the medium in diverse new directions. The only surprise is that it took so long for it to happen! Polymer clay is used by hobbyists, crafters, fine artists, sculptors, doll-makers, miniaturists, animators, illustrators—amateurs and professionals alike.

I am a thoroughly impatient person, so I have always sought out ways of speeding up the making of my polymer clay creations. This book is crammed with the many discoveries that I have made over the years, showing you how to achieve outstanding results with the minimum of effort.

There are over 60 fast polymer clay projects, and virtually all take less than an hour or two to complete. Dozens of techniques are described in clear, step-by-step detail, including short cuts, and there are ideas for variations. The book caters for all abilities: beginners will find the simpler projects provide an entrancing introduction to the craft, and experienced polymer clay artists will be inspired by the wealth of cutting-edge projects and new techniques.

Sue Heaser

Pasta machine (page12)

Pearl and metallic powders
(page 10)

Cutters (page 13)

CHAPTER 1
Materials and equipment

Polymer clay blocks (page 8)

Polymer clay

Polymer clay is sold all over the world under brand names such as Fimo, Sculpey, Premo Sculpey, Cernit, Creall Therm, Du-Kit and Modelene. It is widely available from art and craft stores, toy stores and hobby suppliers.

The popularity of polymer clay has grown hugely in recent years and manufacturers have responded with alacrity. They are constantly improving the quality of their clays and adding new colors, textures and varieties. These range from pearlescent and metallic clays to liquid clays, clays that glow in the dark or under ultraviolet light, clays that are flexible after baking, and clays that simulate semiprecious stones, to mention just a few.

The main properties of polymer clay

All polymer clays have the same main properties:
- Polymer clay is an artificial clay made from small particles of plastic and pigment, suspended in a liquid called a "plasticizer".
- It comes in many different colors, and the clays can be mixed together to make further colors in much the same way as paint.
- It has a very fine texture that allows detailed sculpting and modeling.
- It can be modeled, sculpted, rolled into sheets, applied to armatures, woven, molded, textured, mixed with texturing materials, coated with powdered pigments, stamped and marbled.
- It is baked to a permanent hardness in an ordinary domestic oven set at approximately 275°F (130°C).
- It is non-toxic and when baked, shrinkage or color change is negligible.
- Once baked, most clays are flexible and strong, although baked strength varies between brands.
- It does not dry out in the packet and if stored in a cool place should last for many years, even when the packet has been opened.
- Baked clay can be carved, cut, sanded, polished, added to, baked again, varnished and painted.
- It is used in an enormous variety of ways by artists and craftspeople of all kinds, such as jewelers, sculptors, animators, illustrators, embroiderers, miniaturists and doll-makers.

STORING POLYMER CLAY
If you keep polymer clay cool, it should last for many years. Heat or sunlight will partly bake the clay, and make it hard and unusable. Once a pack of clay is opened, store it in an airtight metal container to prevent it getting dusty. (Avoid plastic containers because the plasticizer in the clay may damage the container.) Wrap clay and millefiori canes in baking parchment or waxed paper (greaseproof paper) before storage.

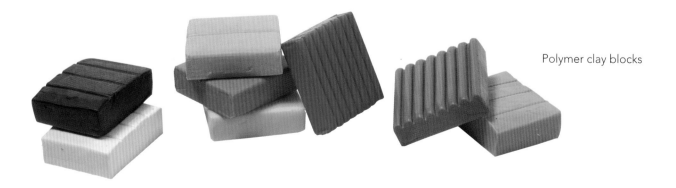

Polymer clay blocks

Types of polymer clay

There are many different varieties of polymer clay:

Colored clay

All brands of polymer clay are sold in a wide range of colors. It is normally sold in small 2oz (65g) blocks of a single color, although larger blocks of 13–18oz (380–500g) are also available. The colors are opaque and brilliant, and can be mixed together to create an enormous palette of colors.

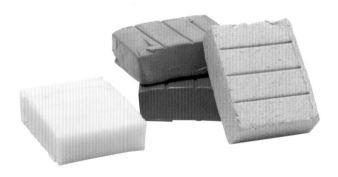

Metallic and pearl clays

The nature of these clays varies. Some have sparkly glitter incorporated into a colored base; others are made with fine mica powder to give a pearly sheen.

Translucent clay

This is sometimes described as "transparent", but in reality is only translucent. It can be tinted with colored clay to produce wonderful frosty pastel colors. It is perfect for making shades for lamps and candles—light glows through it beautifully.

Textured clay

This type of clay is textured with small particles, fiber or glitter and can look remarkably like stone or granite. You can also make your own textured clay by mixing any dry, stable material, such as sand, seeds or dried herbs, into the clay.

Liquid polymer clay

This relatively new product has been seized upon with great delight by many polymer clay designers. The sticky, translucent liquid can be used as a surface glaze, for marbling and enamel effects, to make translucent transfers and for stained-glass effects. It can be colored with oil paint, or powder color can be added to create pearlescent and metallic effects. It normally requires a higher baking temperature than ordinary polymer clay: 300°F (150°C). Use rubbing alcohol (methylated spirit) or a solvent (mineral spirits) for cleaning up.

Specialty clays

Glow-in-the-dark and fluorescent clays can be great fun to use in certain projects. Flexible clay remains flexible after baking, and is ideal for projects where the finished item needs to be capable of bending. It is also useful for making simple molds.

Clay softener

This comes in the form of a liquid or soft clay, and is kneaded into the clay to soften it. There are full instructions for use on the bottle or packet. Softener is useful for salvaging old clay, or for softening clay in order to extrude it through a clay gun.

Other materials

There are many ways to embellish polymer clay, using products such as varnish, paints, pastels, inks and metallic powders. In order to complete the projects, you will need items such as sandpaper, glue, wire and jewelry findings.

Varnish

Gloss varnish is used on baked polymer clay for a shiny surface. Matt varnish protects clay that has been painted where shine is undesirable, such as a doll's face. Use only water-based acrylic varnish, or alcohol-based varnish—other kinds may not dry properly. Polymer clay manufacturers produce their own varnishes and these are guaranteed to be compatible with polymer clay.

Paints

Acrylic paint is the most suitable for polymer clay. (Do not use oil-based enamel paints: they will not dry properly.) It is important to degrease the surface of the clay prior to painting it, so that the paint will adhere well— brush with rubbing alcohol (methylated spirit).

Pearl and metallic powders

These can make the clay look like real silver or gold! Mica powders are available in all sorts of exciting pearl and metallic colors as well as gold, silver and copper.

Artist's pastels

Use soft pastels (not oil or hard pastels) to give subtle colored tints to the clay before baking. These small sticks are on sale in a huge range of colors at art materials suppliers, and can be purchased individually.

Inks

Paint pearlescent inks onto soft polymer clay for exciting crackle effects. Acrylic inks are the best kind to use.

Talcum powder

This is frequently used to prevent clay sticking, especially when using cutters.

Alcohol

Rubbing alcohol (methylated spirits), isopropyl alcohol and denatured alcohol are all ideal for use with polymer clay. They are used for degreasing surfaces—glass and china surfaces before applying clay, baked clay before painting, and metal and baked clay before gluing.

Baking parchment

Baking parchment is excellent for lining cookie sheets (baking sheets) when baking clay, and can be reused many times. It is also excellent for wrapping clay and millefiori canes for storage because it does not absorb plasticizer from the clay.

Aluminum foil

Foil is ideal for making a simple armature for polymer clay. It is also used to support fragile clay creations while they bake, and to cover a former to prevent clay sticking to it.

Wire

Wire is available from hobby suppliers and jewelry-making suppliers. It comes in a wonderful variety of colors and various gauges (diameters). Gauges 18 to 26, or 0.040"–0.016" (1.2mm–0.5mm), are the most useful for polymer clay jewelry.

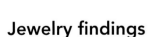

Jewelry findings

This is the term used to describe the various metal attachments necessary to turn polymer clay creations into jewelry, such as necklace clasps, earring backs and brooch pins. Findings come in a variety of finishes, such as silver plate, gilt and hypoallergenic, and are available from hobby stores or jewelry-making suppliers.

Sandpaper

To eliminate bumps and fingerprints, and produce a wonderful sheen, baked polymer clay can be sanded and buffed. Use fine-grade wet-and-dry sandpaper (preferably with a grit size of 600–800), which can be found in home improvement stores or stores selling car accessories. Alternatively, use fine wire wool. To buff clay, use a piece of quilt batting (wadding).

Glues

It is important to use glue that is compatible with polymer clay. Ordinary PVA craft glue is best for gluing soft materials such as paper, fibers and fabric to baked polymer clay. It can also be brushed onto baked clay to provide a key when fresh clay is to be added. Use Superglue to assemble baked clay projects, or for gluing baked clay to jewelry findings.

Equipment

One of the delights of working with polymer clay is that you do not need any specialist equipment—you will probably find that you already have many of the tools at home, in the kitchen or in your sewing workbox.

Workboard

A smooth ceramic tile makes a perfect workboard and can be put straight into the oven with the finished item on it, avoiding the need to move the item and risk damage. The surface should be smooth so that the clay can be stuck down onto it while you work.

Pasta machine

A pasta machine is great for rapidly rolling clay sheets of different thicknesses, conditioning clay before use, or mixing colors. Do not use the machine for food once it has contained polymer clay, because it is impossible to clean it completely.

Cutting tools

A craft knife with a curved blade is extremely versatile and can be used as an appliqué tool as well. Tissue blades are long, straight, very sharp blades, which are invaluable for cutting sheets of clay into strips and rectangles, and for slicing millefiori canes. They are available from polymer clay suppliers (see page 112).

Sculpting and modeling tools

Gather a selection of tools for making holes, sculpting scoring and pricking. Darning needle (1) are perfect for piercing holes in beads. A tapestry or wool needle (2) is my favorite tool for delicate miniature sculpting tasks—look for one that is ⅛" (3mm) thick and has a blunt tip. The metal refill from a ballpoint pen (3) is ideal for making eye sockets in small polymer clay animals. When you buy an artist's paintbrush, the hairs are protected by a little plastic tube. This tube is perfect for making a smiling mouth on the face of a model figure, or for creating the scales on a mermaid or fish (4, 5). A plastic drinking straw could perform the same task. Ball tools (6) can be found at hobby suppliers or cake decorating

Rolling tools

Sheets of clay are a basic requirement for many projects. A glass bottle, or a small nylon or acrylic tube, is easy to use and will not stick to the clay. Place strips of wood or card on either side of the clay as you roll, in order to keep the sheets an even thickness.

1

2

3

4

5

6

7

8

stores, or you can make your own by gluing a round glass bead onto the end of a cocktail stick. Knitting needles and paintbrush handles have many uses (7, 8).

Measuring tools

You will need a ruler to measure the diameter of clay balls, and the length and thickness of clay logs required in the projects. You can make your own simple cardboard measuring template to do this, by cutting notches of differing thicknesses out of the side of a piece of stiff card.

Cutters

Cutters, in a variety of shapes, are available from polymer clay suppliers. Look in kitchenware stores for interesting cookie cutters. Gum paste (sugarcraft) cutters, which are used for cake decorating, are available in small, intricate shapes.

Stamps and texturing tools

Rubber stamps are great fun to use with polymer clay and, when combined with ink or pearl powders, produce sophisticated results extremely quickly. Look out for other stamps such as wooden textile printing stamps (shown right).

Plastic texture sheets are available from polymer clay suppliers. These come in a range of interesting textures, but you can also improvise with fabric, textured wallpaper or any other textured surfaces.

Clay gun (or clay extruder)

Clay guns allow you to create a sausage of clay with varying cross sections. The gun has a selection of discs, each with a different shaped hole through which the clay is ex-truded. It is best to use soft clay in a clay gun.

Baking equipment

To bake your polymer clay projects, use an ovenproof item such as a ceramic tile, cookie sheet (baking sheet) or earthenware dish. If the baking surface is shiny, cover it with baking parchment so that it does not leave a shiny mark on the clay.

A simple kitchen or digital timer is invaluable for reminding you when your project has finished baking.

Jewelry-making equipment

You will need fine-nosed pliers and wire cutters for several of the jewelry projects in this book. To thread beads, use a beading needle or any fine needle.

Using cutters (page 26)

Millefiori canes (page 30)

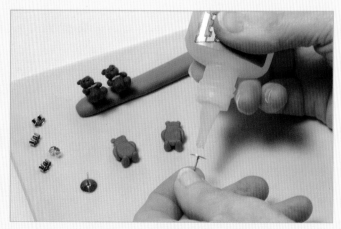

Jewelry techniques (page 32)

CHAPTER 2
Basic techniques

Making basic shapes (page 18)

Preparing the clay

Before you can use polymer clay, it requires a little preparation. This process is often called "conditioning" and involves kneading the clay until it becomes soft and pliable. The following instructions show you how to prepare clay rapidly and efficiently.

Kneading

1 Break or cut off about one quarter of a 2oz (65g) block of clay and roll it between your hands. Some clays are much easier to knead than others—if the clay is quite hard and crumbly, keep pressing the crumbled bits together, rolling and folding the clay as it warms and begins to hold together.

2 After a few minutes, the clay should be fully kneaded. You will know when it is ready because you can bend a log into a U-shape without it cracking. Knead another quarter of the pack and combine with the first, continuing until you have conditioned sufficient clay for the project.

3 Softer clay varieties do not crumble, and can be conditioned rapidly with a pasta machine (see page 12). Cut the clay into thin slices, straight from the pack, and feed them into the pasta machine (set on the widest setting). Fold and repeat until the clay is soft and pliable.

Softening

If the clay is very crumbly, soften it by kneading in a proprietary softening medium such as Fimo Mix Quick or Sculpey Clay Softener.

Leaching

If the clay is too soft, firm it up by allowing some of the plasticizer to leach out (opposite). Roll the clay into a sheet and press it between two sheets of plain white paper. Leave for several hours and then peel off the paper. Some of the oily plasticizer will have been absorbed by the paper and the clay will be much firmer. This is useful for projects with fine detailing.

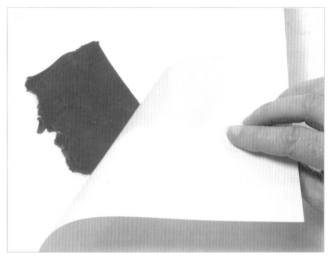

Leaching: peeling off the paper.

SAFETY

Polymer clay is a very safe craft product, and designated as non-toxic. However, as with all craft materials, it is important to take the following simple precautions:

• Wash your hands before and after working with polymer clays.
• Take great care when using tissue blades or other cutting tools.
• Do not allow polymer clay to come into contact with food.
• Polymer clay should not be allowed to burn because it gives off toxic fumes. If you accidentally burn the clay in the oven, turn off the oven, open the windows and leave the room until all traces of the smell have gone.

THE PROJECTS

The projects in this book are suitable for most of the brands of polymer clay. Occasionally, it is necessary to purchase a particular type of clay, in which case it is listed in the materials section.

• Measurements are given throughout—follow these carefully to achieve the best results.
• The clay colors described in the projects are for guidance only, because the colors of different brands vary so much. Descriptive names have been given for colors, rather than the names used by the manufacturers.
• The timing shown for each project is a rough guide and does not include baking time.

Marbling

The technique of marbling produces a delightful streaky effect, which is very decorative. It can be used to simulate marble and wood—particularly useful for dollhouse accessories.

1 Form logs in the required colors. The thickness of each log should correspond to the desired amount of that particular color. Here, pearl white is going to be the main color, so that log is thicker than the black and gold logs. Trim the logs to the same length, press together and roll, keeping the lines of color straight.

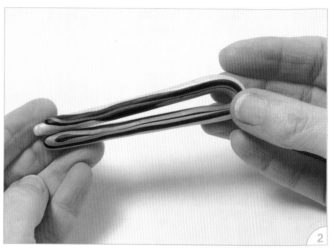

2 Fold the log in half, keeping the lines of color as straight as possible, and roll again. Continue rolling and folding in this way until the lines become fine. Do not continue for too long or all the colors will combine.

3 The marbled log is now ready for use. To make a marbled sheet, place the marbled log on the workboard and roll it flat in the direction of the stripes.

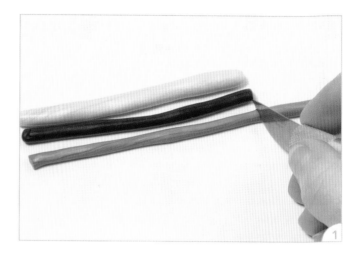

Appliqué

It is possible to create extremely delicate appliqué with polymer clay, reminiscent of fine embroidery. A knife with a curved blade is used to cut and apply tiny slices of clay to a clay base. This technique comes into its own when fingers are too large to work on tiny details, such as the flowers twining up the windmill on page 86.

1 Form a thin log of the shape and thickness required and cut off a slice with the tip of your knife. Scoop the slice onto the blade—the slight tack of the clay will hold it in place. (The photos show a flower being made with appliquéd petals.)

2 Turn the blade over and press the slice on to the clay base. This is easiest if the slice protrudes beyond the tip of the knife, so that you can see it as you position it. The clay base is tackier than the knife blade, so the slice should adhere to the clay. Remove the blade and cut the next slice.

Liquid polymer clay

Liquid clay is a translucent, sticky liquid. On baking, it sets into a tough sheet with a matt surface. It can be colored with oil paints and has many exciting uses (see page 9).

Tinting liquid polymer clay

Pour the liquid clay into a small palette and add a tiny quantity of oil paint on the end of a thick needle. Stir the paint into the clay until all is combined. If the liquid clay becomes too stiff when the paint is added, add a few drops of liquid clay softener (see page 17).

Applying powder colors

Powder colours work beautifully on polymer clays and give surface effects that range from metallic and iridescent through to soft and subtle pastels.

Metallic and pearlescent powders

Brush the powder onto the unbaked clay surface with a soft paintbrush. Bake as usual and then protect the powder with a coat of gloss varnish for maximum shine. To highlight raised areas on textured surfaces, apply powder with your fingertips.

Artist's soft pastels

Rub the pastel on a sheet of paper and then use a soft paintbrush to scoop up the resulting powder and brush it over the soft clay. This technique is very effective for creating a realistic "browned" effect on miniature food such as roast chicken. It is also ideal for applying soft areas of color to flower petals or dolls' cheeks.

Using cutters

Cutters are quick and easy to use and make short work of cutting out regular shapes. The following method ensures that the cutters do not stick to the clay, and the cut-out pieces are free from distortion.

1 Roll out a sheet of clay on a tile, pressing it down lightly so that it sticks to the tile. Brush a little talcum powder over the surface of the clay. Press the cutter into the clay.

2 Gently pull away the waste clay, leaving the cut-out shapes on the tile. Carefully remove the shapes from the tile with the blade of a knife.

Turning a wire loop

It is often necessary to turn a neat loop in the end of a piece of wire when assembling jewelry.

1 Grip the end of the wire in fine-nosed pliers, positioning the wire at a point on the pliers' tapered jaws that is the size of the loop you require. Turn the pliers right around to form a loop.

2 Remove the pliers and replace them in the loop so that you can turn the loop backwards a little to position it centrally at the end of the wire. Squeeze the loop shut with your pliers or leave it open in order to attach another loop.

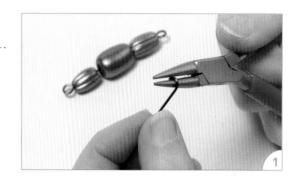

Stringing a necklace

1 Thread a beading needle with twice the required length of beading thread and double it, tying a knot in the end. Thread the beads, and when you reach the final bead, tie another knot and slip a second needle into the knot's loop. Hold the thread taut with the beading needle and use the other needle to pull the knot down tightly on top of the last bead.

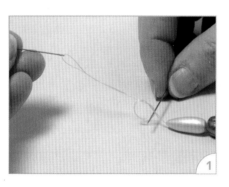

2 Take a calotte crimp and use your pliers to squeeze the two halves of it over the knot, so that the beading thread emerges from the last bead into the bottom of the crimp and the knot is enclosed

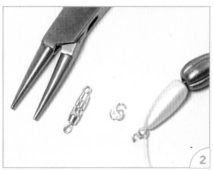

inside. A drop of Superglue on each knot will make it more secure. Trim the trailing end of the thread. Repeat for the other end of the necklace. Attach a clasp to the loops on the calottes.

Attaching a pendant bail

Pendant bails are small loops of metal that are squeezed onto a hole in a pendant and provide an attachment point for a chain. When making a polymer clay pendant, take care to make the hole the right size for the bail. After baking, use pliers to squeeze the claws of the bail on to the hole.

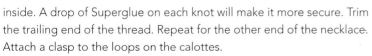

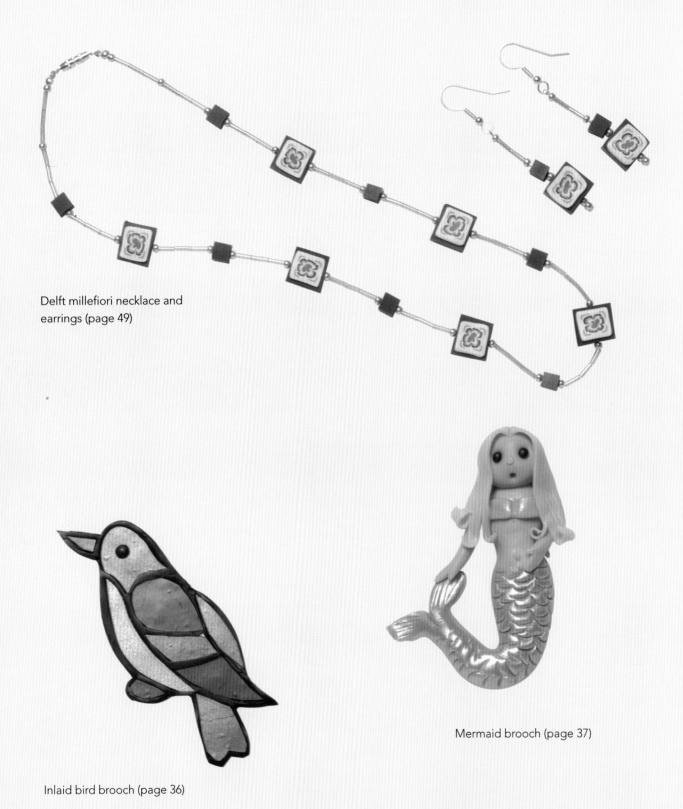

Delft millefiori necklace and earrings (page 49)

Inlaid bird brooch (page 36)

Mermaid brooch (page 37)

CHAPTER 3
Jewelry

Top: Rose stick pin (page 38)

Bottom: Teddy bear ear studs (page 45)

Brooches

Inlaid bird brooch

Pearly sheets of baked clay are cut to shape and pressed into a black clay background to make this striking brooch. The technique resembles marquetry or pietre dure mosaics, but is far quicker and easier than either.

🕐 30 minutes

Template: see page 106

TOOLS Pasta machine or a roller • Ceramic tile • Craft knife • Tracing paper and pencil • Small pair of sharp scissors • Brooch pin

MATERIALS Polymer clay, 2oz (65g) blocks: ¼ block black, ⅛ block pearl, ⅛ block copper, ⅛ block gold • Superglue

1 Use the pasta machine or roller to roll out the pearl clay into a thin sheet about 1/32" (1mm) thick and 2" (5cm) square. Repeat for the copper and gold clays. Smooth the sheets onto a tile, ensuring that there are no air bubbles under the clay, and bake for 30 minutes. Remove from the tile.

2 Trace the template onto tracing paper. Rub over the back with a soft pencil and transfer the shapes to the baked sheets of copper, pearl and gold. Cut out the shapes with the scissors. If the clay crumbles, it is not baked enough so return it to the oven for a further 20 minutes.

3 Roll out a sheet of black clay, about 1/16" (1.5mm) thick, and place it on a tile. Arrange the cut-out pieces on this to make up the shape of the bird, but keep them slightly apart. Run the roller firmly over the top of the pieces until they are flush with the surrounding clay.

4 Cut neatly around the outside of the bird with the craft knife, leaving a border of black 1/16" (1.5mm) wide. Bake the piece on the tile for 30 minutes. When it is cool, remove from the tile and glue a brooch pin to the back.

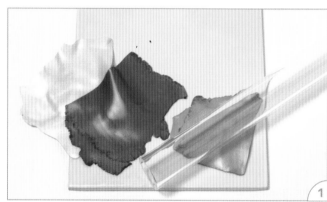

MORE IDEAS

Make a butterfly in the same way, using pearl clay tinted with blue, green and purple. Take care to cut the opposite wing pieces identically for a symmetrical result. Create a flower by applying colored foils to a sheet of black clay before baking.

> **TIP**
> *Use carbon or transfer paper to speed up the process of transferring the design onto the clay sheets.*

Mermaid brooch

A dreamy mermaid with a pearly tail makes an unusual brooch. Instead of a brooch pin, you could glue a magnet to the back to make a fridge magnet. For a really sparkly tail, different colors of pearlescent powder could be used.

 30 minutes

TOOLS Craft knife • Ceramic tile • Tapestry needle • Brush protector • Pointed tool • Pasta machine or roller • Brooch pin
MATERIALS Polymer clay, 2oz (65g) blocks: ¼ block light flesh, small amounts of translucent yellow and turquoise (see mixtures below) • Pearlescent powder: blue-green or silver • Gloss varnish
MIXTURES To make translucent turquoise: ¼" (6mm) ball of translucent, trace of turqoise. To make translucent yellow: ½" (13mm) ball of translucent, trace of yellow

1 Form a ¾" (20mm) ball of light flesh clay. Roll this into a log, about 3⅛" (8cm) long, tapered at one end. Cut a slit, ½" (13mm) long, in the center of the tapered end. Flatten the log and pinch a waist about ½" (13mm) from the top. Curve the tail and splay the ends to form the tail fin.

2 Mark lines on the fin and press the end of the brush protector all over the tail to suggest scales. Brush the tail with blue-green powder. Form a log of translucent turquoise clay, ¹⁄₁₆" (1.5mm) thick, and roll this flat for the bikini top.

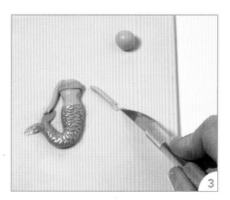

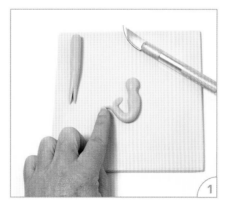

3 Position the bikini top, trimming it to fit and mark a cleavage. Form two logs of flesh for the arms, ⅛" (3mm) thick and 1" (25mm) long, with rounded ends. Make hands—flatten one end and cut out a notch. Use a ½" (13mm) ball of flesh for the head.

4 To make the hair, roll the translucent yellow clay into a sheet ⅜" (10mm) wide and 2¾" (7cm) long. Fringe and curl the ends. Make eye sockets filled with black clay. Apply a tiny flesh nose and mark a mouth. Bake for 30 minutes. Varnish the powder and glue on the brooch back.

Rose stick pins

Roses are eternally popular motifs in jewelry and these dainty stick pins can be made in a glorious variety of colors and effects. Wear them on lapels or a hat to experience summer at any time of year.

🕐 20 minutes

TOOLS Ceramic tile • Craft knife • Stick pin with a flat pad and protector
MATERIALS Polymer clay: small amount of crimson and leaf green
• Superglue

1 Form the leaf green clay into a log, ¼" (6mm) thick, and cut two ⅛" (3mm) lengths. Shape each of these into a teardrop and press it down firmly on the tile to flatten it into a leaf shape. Mark veins with the knife and cut under each leaf to free it from the tile. Press the leaves together at a slight angle.

2 Form a log of crimson clay, ¼" (6mm) thick, and cut a ¼" (6mm) length. Shape this into a cone and press it down on the tile. Cut seven lengths, ⅛" (3mm) long. Form these into balls and pinch one into a thin petal about ⅜" (10mm) in diameter. Wrap this around the cone.

3 Make another petal in the same way and wrap this around the other side of the cone. Continue making and adding petals, working around the rose. Pull the tops of the outer petals outwards. Trim the base of the rose and press it on top of the leaves. Bake for 20 minutes. When the rose is cool, glue it to the stick pin pad.

MORE IDEAS
Try making roses in different colors. Use pearl clay to make a pearly pink rose, brushing it with pink and green pearlescent powders. Use copper clay to make a coppery gold rose, thickly applying gold powder to the leaves, and more sparingly to the petals.

Feather brooches

Stylish and unusual, these exotic brooches resemble fluttering feathers or the waving fronds of sea anemones. You can vary the colors of the clay sheets, but make sure that they are in strongly contrasting colors.

 30 minutes

TOOLS Pasta machine or roller • Tissue blade or sharp knife • Ceramic tile • Brooch pin
MATERIALS Polymer clay, 2oz (65g) blocks: ¼ block beige; ¼ block dark brown; ¼ block white • Superglue

1 Roll out a sheet of beige clay ¹⁄₁₆" (1.5mm) thick, and trim it to make a rectangle 3" x 2"(7.5cm x 5cm). Repeat for the other two clay colors. Stack the rectangles with the brown in the middle and roll up to make a spiral cane.

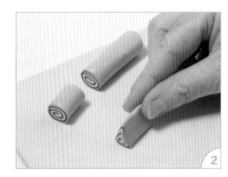

2 Reduce the cane to ¾" (20mm) in diameter (see page 28). Cut off ¾" (20mm), place it on the tile and squeeze the top to give it a triangular cross-section. Mark the center with a line. Using the tissue blade, make a cut, ¹⁄₃₂" (1mm) from one end, almost to the bottom of the cane.

MORE IDEAS
Try using colors to match a favorite outfit. The slices can be pressed down in a variety of ways

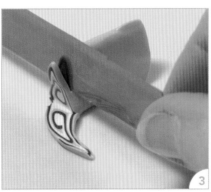

> **TIP**
> *If the cane squashes as you slice it, chill it in the refrigerator for about 10 minutes.*

3 Pull down the resulting flap, curving it downwards 90°, and press it lightly to the tile. Repeat to cut further ¹⁄₃₂" (1mm) flaps, pressing each over the previous flap at a shallower angle until there are about seven in a gentle curve, and you have almost reached the center of the length of cane.

4 To make a symmetrical design, repeat for the other side. As you work into the center, alternate the flaps up and down, keeping the two sides symmetrical. Bake the piece on the tile for 30 minutes. When it is cool, glue the brooch pin to the back.

Buttons

Scrimshaw buttons

During the age of sailing ships, sailors would decorate, carve or engrave bone, shells and ivory as a leisure activity—a craft called scrimshaw. Polymer clay simulates ivory very effectively and these pretty buttons copy scrimshaw techniques. The buttons should be handwashed because of the applied paint.

 45 minutes   Template: see page 106

TOOLS Craft knife • Ceramic tile • Talcum powder • A marble • Tapestry needle • Pencil • Darning needle or sharp point for engraving • Paintbrush • Fine wire wool or 600 grit sandpaper

MATERIALS Polymer clay, 2oz (65g) blocks: ¼ block beige (Premo Ecru), ¼ block translucent, ¼ block white • Tracing paper • Rubbing alcohol (methylated spirit) • Acrylic paint: black, blue, red, yellow • Matt varnish

1 Marble the three clays (see page 24) until the streaks are fine, and make a log, ⅜" (10mm) thick. Cut this into 1" (25mm) lengths. Form each length into a ball and press down on the tile to make discs 1" (25mm) in diameter. Stroke talc over each disc and indent the center with the marble. Pierce four holes in the center of each indentation with the tapestry needle.

2 Bake the buttons on the tile for 30 minutes. When cool, trace the template and transfer the design to the buttons. Scribe over the lines with the darning needle, working over each line several times to ensure it is deeply engraved.

3 Brush rubbing alcohol (methylated spirit) over each button and let it dry. Brush black acrylic paint over the scribed design, working it into the lines. Leave to dry completely. Remove the excess with wire wool. The scribed lines will appear as thin black lines.

4 Tint the flowers with thin washes of acrylic paint. Leave to dry thoroughly, then coat the buttons with matt varnish.

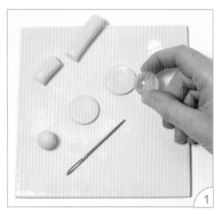

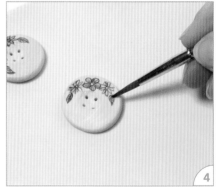

TIP
To make neat holes in buttons, pierce straight down with a tapestry needle until it touches the workboard, then rotate the needle in the hole to enlarge it.

Ladybug buttons

Ladybugs are always a favorite with children. These cheerful buttons would look delightful marching up the front of a hand-knitted cardigan. Make sure that you bake the buttons well so that they are really strong. These buttons can be machine-washed on a cool cycle.

 30 minutes

TOOLS Craft knife • Ceramic tile • Tapestry needle
MATERIALS Polymer clay, 2oz (65g) blocks: ¼ block red, scraps of black and yellow

1 Make all the buttons at the same time for uniformity. Roll a log ⅜" (10mm) thick and cut slices ³⁄₁₆" (5mm) thick for each button. Shape these into ovals and press them on the tile until they are ½" (13mm) across and an even shape.

2 Make a log of black clay ⅛" (3mm) thick and cut ⅛" (3mm) slices for the heads. Shape these into ovals and press on the bodies. Indent a line down the center of each body.

3 Form a log of black, ¹⁄₁₆" (1.5mm) thick. For each ladybug, cut and appliqué seven thin slices on the body to form the spots (see page 25), using the photograph as a guide. Repeat the process with yellow clay to apply eyes to the head. Make two holes in each button, on the center line, and bake on the tile for 30 minutes.

MORE IDEAS

Try making ladybugs in different colors and sizes. To make beetle buttons, use black clay, omit the spots, and brush with pearlescent powders. Varnish after baking and always make sure the buttons are handwashed. These beetles have lines scribed on their wings for more sparkle.

TIP
To ensure even spots on the ladybugs, use a firm clay for the appliqué or leach the clay before you begin (see page 17).

Earrings, rings and bracelets

Lemon tree drop earrings

These juicy earrings use the lemon slice millefiori canes from page 28, applied to simple round beads. Drop earrings are quick and easy to make and you can use tiny glass beads to add sparkle to the clay.

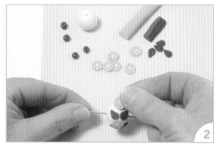

30 minutes, using a pre-made cane

TOOLS Craft knife • Darning needle • Tissue blade • Fine-nosed pliers
MATERIALS Polymer clay, 2oz (65g) blocks: ¼ block white, scrap of leaf green • 1 lemon slice millefiori cane (see page 28), 1 leaf millefiori cane (see page 29) • 2 silver-plated head pins: 2" (5cm) • 6 small yellow glass beads • 2 silver glass bugle beads • 2 silver-plated French (fish-hook) ear wires

1 Make a log of white clay, ½" (13mm) thick, and cut two 1" (25mm) lengths. Make two large white beads following the instructions on page 19. Form a log of leaf green, ⅛" (3mm) thick, and cut four ⅛" (3mm) lengths. Use these to make four small beads.

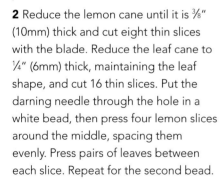

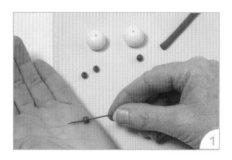

2 Reduce the lemon cane until it is ⅜" (10mm) thick and cut eight thin slices with the blade. Reduce the leaf cane to ¼" (6mm) thick, maintaining the leaf shape, and cut 16 thin slices. Put the darning needle through the hole in a white bead, then press four lemon slices around the middle, spacing them evenly. Press pairs of leaves between each slice. Repeat for the second bead.

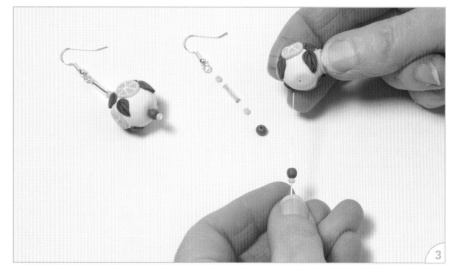

3 Bake the beads for 20 minutes. When cool, thread onto the head pins in the order shown. Turn a loop in the top of the head pin (see page 33). Attach a French (fish-hook) wire to each loop.

MORE IDEAS
Reduce the lemon cane to ½" (13mm) in diameter. Cut two ⅛" (3mm) slices and pierce them horizontally. Make two ⅛" (3mm) leaf green beads. Bake the beads and slices. Thread onto head pins as above, adding small yellow glass beads to accent the colors.

TIP
Trim each head pin to ¼" (6mm) above the top bead. This will be about the right length for making the loop.

Spiral rings

Wire is available in many exciting colors today and this stylish spiral ring features a striking combination of a green wire with a violet clay stone. The ring can be made to fit any size.

 15 minutes per ring

TOOLS Former: the barrel of a thick pen, a tube of lipstick or a similar round shape about the thickness of your finger • Fine-nosed pliers • Small paintbrush • Wire cutters
MATERIALS Polymer clay: scrap of black clay • Green metallic wire (18–20 gauge) • Masking tape • Pearlescent powder: violet • Superglue • Gloss varnish

1 Cut an 8" (20cm) length of wire. Place the center of this on the former and wrap each end once around the former.

2 Cover the jaws of the pliers with masking tape to prevent them marking the wire. Make a loop in one end of the wire and keep winding it round, forming a horizontal spiral. Repeat with the other end, coiling until the spirals are opposite each other. Adjust the ring to fit.

3 Form a ⅛" (3mm) ball of black clay, and press it in the center of one of the spirals until it flattens into a round, domed "stone". Brush the clay with violet powder. Bake the ring for 20 minutes. When cool, squeeze a drop of glue on the back of the stone to secure it and varnish over the powder.

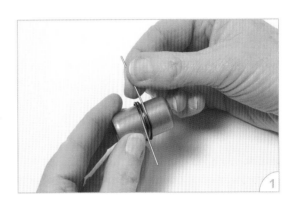

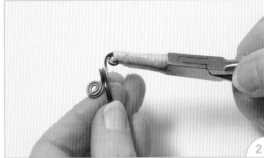

MORE IDEAS
Try combining copper wire with two stones of marbled blue, turquoise and purple clay. Red metallic wire looks great set against stones made of marbled green and pearl clays. After baking, varnish all stones for extra sparkle.

> **TIP**
> *To adjust the ring size, ease the wire into a tighter or looser coil by pushing the spirals together or apart.*

Hair accessories

Mosaic barrette

Polymer clay is ideal for creating wonderful mosaics. This striking barrette was inspired by the mosaics of ancient Rome. Pre-baked clay tiles are laid on a black clay ground—fast, fun and unusual.

 1 hour　　　　　　　　　　　　Template: see page 106

TOOLS Pasta machine or roller • Ceramic tile • Graph paper • Darning needle • Tissue blade or sharp knife • Spreader or piece of card
MATERIALS Polymer clay, 2oz (65g) blocks: ¼ block white, ¼ block black, ⅛ block leaf green, ⅛ block red, small quantity of golden yellow • Liquid polymer clay • Barrette • Superglue

1 Roll the white clay into a sheet, ¹⁄₁₆" (1.5mm) thick and 3" (7.5cm) square. Put it on the tile and place the graph paper over it. Use the needle to prick through the paper and impress a grid on the clay at ¼" (6mm) intervals.

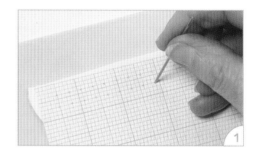

2 Remove the graph paper and cut along the lines of the grid with the blade to make the mosaic squares. Remove waste clay from around the squares and leave them on the tile for baking. Repeat with the leaf green, red and yellow clays. Bake for 30 minutes.

3 When cool, remove the squares from the tile, snapping them apart along the cutting lines if necessary. Roll out a sheet of black clay on the tile, ¹⁄₁₆" (1.5mm) thick. Cut the top edge straight and use it as a guideline. Press rows of mosaic squares into the black clay, spaced slightly apart, starting at the top edge and following the design template.

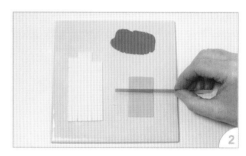

4 Trim around the edges of the mosaic. Spread liquid polymer clay over the surface to mimic grout, working it into the spaces with the spreader. Wipe with a cloth to remove the excess. Bake on the tile for 30 minutes. When cool, glue the barrette to the back, flexing the mosaic to fit the curve.

MORE IDEAS
Mosaic tiles can be made in a wide range of colors, perhaps with marbled effects, and incorporated into many designs. Simple designs are the most effective.

TIP
Consider making plenty of extra mosaic tiles, so that you can use them to create other mosaic jewelry such as earrings and pendants. Apply the tiles to a backing sheet of soft clay in the same way.

Gilded plait barrette

Simple twists of black clay, gleaming with gold and copper powders, make this barrette look like real metal. When the piece is tilted back and forth, the alternating twists produce a delightful illusion of movement.

 30 minutes

TOOLS Pasta machine or roller • Ceramic tile • Tissue blade • Ruler • Soft paintbrush • Barrette
MATERIALS Polymer clay, 2oz (65g) blocks: ½ block black • Pearlescent powder: gold, copper • Gloss varnish

1 Roll out a sheet of black clay, ¹⁄₁₂" (2mm) thick. Place it on the tile and, using the rule, cut a rectangle measuring 1" x 3½" (2.5cm x 9cm). Remove waste clay from around the rectangle.

2 Roll out another sheet of the same thickness, 4" (10cm) long, and use the tissue blade to cut strips ¹⁄₁₂" (2mm) wide. Press one end of a strip on top of one end of the rectangle, and twist the strip until it is evenly twisted along its length. Press down the end. Repeat with the next strip, applying it just below the first and twisting it in the opposite direction.

3 Repeat to make a total of six strips, each twisted in the opposite direction to the previous one. Trim any excess clay on the bottom edge. Trim the ends of the rectangle to neaten them.

4 Brush alternating bands of copper and gold powder diagonally across the rectangle. Bake for 30 minutes and when cool, varnish with gloss varnish to protect the powder. Glue the rectangle to the barrette, flexing it to fit the curve.

> **TIP**
> *Be careful not to inhale pearlescent and metallic powders: use a dust-mask.*

Necklaces and pendants

Pearly bead necklace

Pearlescent powders look gorgeous on polymer clay and this project combines colored pearly beads with wire and chain for a truly opulent necklace. A pair of pearl drop earrings completes the set.

 1 hour

TOOLS Craft knife • Magnifying glass or a clear plastic box lid • Darning needle • Soft paintbrush • Fine-nosed pliers • Wire cutters

MATERIALS Polymer clay, 2oz (65g) blocks: ¼ block white; ½ block black • Pearlescent powder: white, violet, blue, green • Gloss varnish • Gold-plated wire (22 gauge) • Gold-plated trace chain, 12" (30cm) long

1 Make a log of black clay, ½" (13 mm) thick, and cut five ½" (13 mm) lengths. Roll each into a ball, place it on a smooth surface and put the magnifying glass over it. Pressing gently, rotate the glass horizontally and you will see the bead forming—this shape of bead is termed bicone.

2 Pierce each bead through its points, taking care not to distort the symmetrical shape. (See page 32 for how to pierce beads.) Now make eight round beads, ¼" (6mm) in diameter, from white clay (see page 30). Brush the white beads with white pearlescent powder and the black beads with colored powders. Bake all the beads for 30 minutes.

3 Coat each bead with gloss varnish to protect the powder. Thread each bead on a length of wire, turning a loop at each end (see page 33). Assemble the beads in the order shown. Cut the center of the chain and attach each end to the string of linked beads.

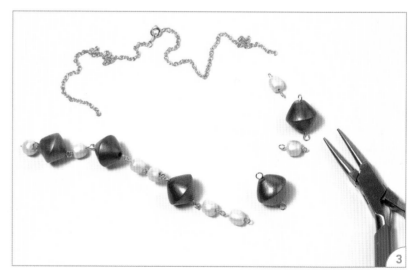

TIP
To make varnishing easier, thread beads on a length of wire. Bend a hook in the end of the wire and hang up the beads to dry.

MORE IDEAS
To make the pearl drop earrings shown above: form two teardrops of white clay and pierce them longitudinally. Brush with white pearlescent powder, then bake and varnish as above. Thread each bead on a length of wire, turning a spiral at the bottom of the drop (see page 43) and a loop at the top. Attach French (fish-hook) ear wires.

Delft millefiori necklace

A beautiful necklace in sumptuous blues, using the Delft millefiori cane on page 30 (for a different look, substitute any other cane). A fast threading technique, plus long bugle beads, allow the necklace to be put together speedily.

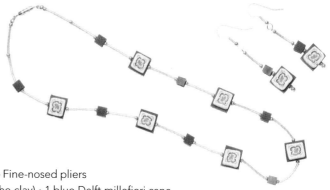

 1 hour

TOOLS Tissue blade or sharp knife • Darning needle • Fine beading needle • Fine-nosed pliers
MATERIALS Polymer clay, 2oz (65g) blocks: 1 block blue pearl (do not knead the clay) • 1 blue Delft millefiori cane (see page 30)
• Strong white polyester thread, or beading silk • 48 blue glass bugle beads, ⅜" (10mm) long • 30 round, silver glass beads, ⅛" (3mm) in diameter • 2 silver-plated calotte crimps • Silver-plated necklace clasp

1 Put the unkneaded clay on your workboard and use the tissue blade to cut a rectangular block from one end, ½" (13mm) thick and square in section. Trim all the edges. Cut six slices, ⅛" (3mm) thick, from the end of the block. Cut two more slices, ¼" (6mm) thick and cut each of these into four to make the small, square beads.

2 Reduce the cane until it is a little smaller in section than the blue slices. Cut thin slices from it and press them on both sides of the blue slices. Use the darning needle to pierce a hole through the center of each bead, taking care not to split the clay. Pierce the small, square beads in the same way. Bake all the beads for 30 minutes.

3 Using a doubled thread, 18" (55cm) long and knotted at the end, thread the beads in the order shown. Knot the second end of the thread and use the pliers to nip a calotte crimp over each of the two end knots (see page 33). Attach a clasp to the calotte loops.

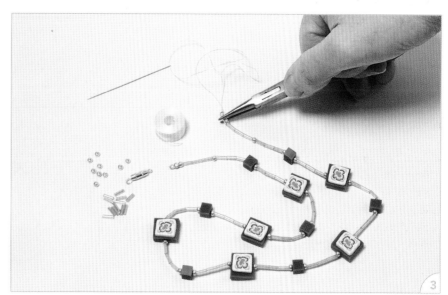

MORE IDEAS
The earrings pictured are made in the same way as the Lemon Tree Drop Earrings on page 42.

TIP
If you do not have a beading needle, stiffen the end of the thread with glue to make threading easier.

Jade tooth pendant

Polymer clay is wonderful for simulating semiprecious stones, and this faux jade pendant is remarkably realistic. A leather thong helps confirm the illusion of a weighty stone.

🕐 30 minutes

TOOLS Grater • Darning needle • Knitting needle • Ceramic tile • Craft knife
MATERIALS Polymer clay, 2oz (65g) blocks: ¼ block translucent, small scraps of leaf green and black (the black should be unkneaded) • Fine sandpaper (600–800 grit) • Scrap of quilt batting (wadding) • Copper wire (18–20 gauge): 6"(15cm) long • Leather thong: 24" (60cm) long and 1⁄32" (1mm) thick

1 Mix a 3⁄8"(10mm) ball of leaf green clay into the translucent clay until the colors are streaky. Grate the mixture through the large holes in the grater. Finely grate a little black clay. Gather together the green gratings with a few of the black specks, and form them into a ball.

2 Form the ball into a log, ½" (13mm) thick and tapering to a point. With the knitting needle, make a groove 1½" (4cm) from the point and 3⁄16" (5mm) wide (see page 20). Pierce a hole through the tooth with the darning needle, 1⁄16" (1.5mm) in diameter and about ¼" (6mm) above the groove.

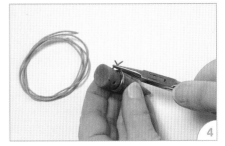

MORE IDEAS
Try using granite, or other stone-effect clay. Vary the colors of the wire wrap and the leather thong.

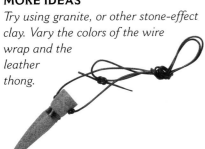

3 Bake the tooth for 30 minutes. While it is still warm, cut off the rounded top to give it a sharp edge. Sand down the tooth with sandpaper and buff it to a shine with the quilt batting (wadding)— see page 27.

4 Wrap the wire around the groove, twisting the ends together at the back to tighten the coil. Trim the ends and press them flush with the back. Thread the thong through the hole, knotting it on either side of the tooth. Knot the end of the thong.

> **TIP**
> *Polymer clay is easier to grate if you chill it in the refrigerator beforehand.*

Stamped lapis pendant

Rubber stamps work beautifully on polymer clay and this lovely pendant simulates the deep blue of lapis lazuli, a semiprecious stone. It is worth keeping a lookout for small rubber stamps to add to your jewelry-making tools—simple designs with clear shapes are the best.

 15 minutes

TOOLS Grater • Tapestry needle • Ceramic tile • Small rubber stamp in a design of your choice
MATERIALS Polymer clay, 65g/2oz blocks: ¼ block ultramarine blue, scraps of translucent • Pearlescent powder: gold • Fine sandpaper (600–800 grit) • Quilt batting (wadding) • Pendant bail (gilt) • Large jump ring (gilt) • Chain (gilt): length to suit

1 Finely grate the translucent clay to make some tiny flecks. Form a ball of blue clay, ⅝" (15mm) in diameter, and roll it in the translucent specks so that some specks are picked up on the surface. Roll the ball to smooth in the specks, then shape it into a teardrop.

2 Press the teardrop on the tile with the flat of your finger until it is about ¼" (6mm) thick. Smooth the surface and edges to make a symmetrical pendant drop. Smear a coating of gold powder over the surface of the stamp with your fingertip, shake off any excess and stamp into the clay.

3 Make a hole in the top of the pendant with the tapestry needle and bake it on the tile for 30 minutes. Sand the surface of the pendant (the recessed stamped image will not be affected) and buff it to a shine with the batting (wadding). Attach a pendant bail to the hole, with a jump ring to take the chain.

MORE IDEAS
To make a jade pendant, use the recipe for faux jade opposite. Press the stamp into a black inkpad before stamping.

TIP
Before baking, lightly stroke the surface of the pendant with your fingertip. This will burnish the clay to a sheen and make sanding easier after baking.

Dollhouse food (page 54)

Dollhouse accessories (page 62)

Dollhouse pets (page 60)

CHAPTER 4

Miniatures

All the miniatures in this chapter are in the standard dollhouse scale of 1:12 or 1":1ft.

Top: Cat (page 61)
Bottom: Fruit (page 57)

Dollhouse food

Chocolate cake

Polymer clay is excellent for making miniature food because it can simulate many textures and achieve accurate colors. These mini cakes will make your mouth water and can be "baked" in moments.

 10 minutes per cake

TOOLS Large tapestry needle • Craft knife • Ceramic tile
MATERIALS Polymer clay: small amounts of dark brown and ochre

1 Form a ¾" (20mm) ball of brown clay, and flatten it until it is about ⅜" (10mm) thick. Roll to straighten the sides and place on the tile.

2 Form a ¼" (6mm) ball of well-kneaded brown clay. Flatten it into a thin disc to make the icing for the cake. With the eye of the needle, mark wavy lines across the surface. Slice under the icing with your knife to free it from the tile and pat it on top of the cake.

3 Form a long thin log of ochre clay, about 1/32" (1mm) thick and 4" (10cm) long. Fold it in half and twist the ends to make a miniature rope. Wrap around the base of the cake and around the top edge, to cover the edge of the icing. Bake the cake on the tile for 20 minutes.

MORE IDEAS

To make a strawberry cake, use white clay for the cake and the twisted decoration. Make strawberries by forming 1/16" (1.5mm) balls of crimson clay, and pointing one end slightly. Arrange them in the center of the cake and prick with a pin to texture.

To make a lemon cake, mix a little yellow clay into the translucent clay and use this for the cake. Reduce the lemon cane to 1/16 in (1.5mm) thick and cut tiny slices. Make little teardrops of white clay. Press these decorations on top of the cake.

> **TIP**
> *To make platters for the cakes, use a circular cutter to cut 1"(25mm) circles from a thin sheet of white clay rolled out on a tile. Bake, remove from the tile and turn over.*

Roast chicken

This succulent roast chicken would make an impressive centerpiece for a dollhouse dinnertable. To create that fresh-from-the oven look, artist's pastels have been used, together with a smear of varnish to give a sheen.

 15 minutes

TOOLS Craft knife • Ceramic tile • Blunt tapestry needle • Soft paintbrush
MATERIALS Polymer clay, 2oz (65g) blocks: ⅛ block beige • Artist's pastels: ochre, burnt sienna (reddish brown) • Gloss varnish

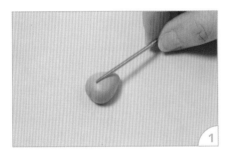

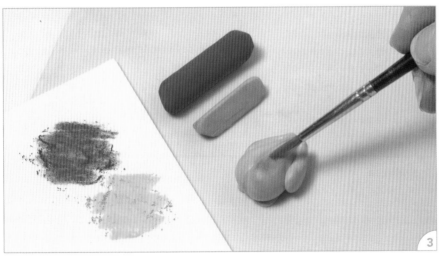

1 To make the body of the chicken, form a ⅝" (15mm) ball of beige clay, and point one end a little. With the needle, indent the blunt end with a vertical line for the breast and mark lightly along the center line of the body. Make a horizontal slit in the pointed end.

2 To make the wings, form two logs, 1/16" (1.5mm) thick and about ¾" (20mm) long. Fold over one end of each. Press these on the tile about ¼" (6mm) apart, with the folded ends pointing inwards. Press the body on top so that the wings just protrude below the breast.

3 To make the legs, form two 5/16" (8mm) balls of clay, and shape them into teardrops. Roll the thin end between your fingers to make an indentation just before the end of the leg. Press the legs on the chicken. Brush the bird lightly with ochre and burnt sienna pastels (see page 10). Bake for 15 minutes. Coat sparingly with gloss varnish to suggest a film of grease.

MORE IDEAS
To make chicken drumsticks, follow Step 3 above and then brown and varnish in the same way. To make sausages, add a touch of crimson clay to the beige and shape into sausages ¼" (6mm) long. Apply artist's pastels, bake and then varnish.

TIP
To make miniature roast potatoes, cut mini potatoes (see page 56) in half and brown them with pastels in the same way. Bake and varnish.

Vegetables

Growing your own miniature vegetables is great fun with polymer clay. The clay forms easily into the rounded shapes and any irregularities just make the vegetables look more organic!

 5–10 minutes for each type of vegetable

TOOLS Craft knife • Needle • Pin • Paintbrush • Ceramic tile
MATERIALS
CARROTS: Polymer clay: a ⅝" (15mm) ball of orange
POTATOES: Polymer clay: a ⅝" (15mm) ball of beige • Artist's pastel: brown
CABBAGES: Polymer clay: a ½" (13mm) ball each of leaf green and pale leaf green
MIXTURES To make pale leaf green: 1 part leaf green, 1 part yellow

1 Carrots
Form a ³⁄₁₆" (5mm) ball of orange clay, and roll to shape it into a pointed cone. Hold the knife blade across the carrot and roll it back and forth to make lots of short lines along the length of the carrot. Indent the center of the carrot top with the needle. Bake as below.

2 Potatoes
Form balls of beige clay, between ¹⁄₁₆" (1.5mm), and ⅛" (3mm) across and shape these into irregular ovals. Make "eyes" with the pinhead. Brush the potatoes with brown pastel (see page 10). Bake as below.

3 Cabbages
Form the pale leaf green into a ⅜" (10mm) ball for the cabbage heart. Form three ⅛" (3mm) balls of pale leaf green, and pinch each into an oval leaf shape. Wrap these around the heart. Make several slightly larger leaves of leaf green, indent the edges with the needle and mark veins. Wrap around the cabbage, turning the edges out slightly. Bake all the vegetables for 15 minutes.

MORE IDEAS
To make parsnips, follow the method for carrots, using an equal mix of white and beige clays. Make the parsnips a little larger than the carrots. To make a cauliflower, follow the method for cabbage, but make the head with white clay and indent with the needle to texture it. (both pictured top)

> **TIP**
> *Use firm (or well-leached, see page 17) clay for all miniatures, or the heat from your hands will make such small quantities of clay too soft to model successfully.*

Fruit

Apples, pears, oranges and bananas – this collection of mini fruit would make a splendid display in a dollhouse kitchen. When making dollhouse food, take care to keep the clay colors muted for a realistic effect.

 5 minutes for each type of fruit

TOOLS Craft knife • Fine wire brush or a toothbrush • Needle • Paintbrush • Ceramic tile

MATERIALS
ORANGES: Polymer clay: a ⅝" (15mm) ball of orange
APPLES: Polymer clay: a ⅜" (10mm) ball each of green, golden yellow and white combined to make apple green
BANANAS: Polymer clay: a ⅝" (15mm) ball of yellow • Artist's pastel: black
PEARS: Polymer clay: a ⅝" (15mm) ball of gold

MORE IDEAS
To make red apples, use a mixture of yellow and white clays and brush the sides of the apples with crimson pastel to give streaks.

1 Oranges
Form several ¼" (6mm) balls of orange clay, and roll them on the bristles of the brush to texture them. Make a small hole in each with the needle to imitate the stalk end.

2 Apples and pears
Form ¼" (6mm) balls of apple green clay for the apples. Pierce a hole to imitate the stalk end. Repeat with the gold clay to make pears, pinching them into a pear shape.

3 Bananas
Form several ¼" (6mm) balls of yellow clay, roll each into a short log with rounded ends, and curve into a banana shape. Press the bananas together into a bunch. To suggest ripeness, apply the black artist's pastel powder to the sides of the bananas with a fine brush. Bake all the fruit for 20 minutes.

Chocolate bar

A tiny bar of milk chocolate, wrapped in gold paper, looks very appealing. You could also try making it in a creamy white or a darker brown, to suggest white and plain chocolate respectively. Miniature chocolates and candies are probably as addictive to make as their real-life counterparts are to eat.

 10 minutes

TOOLS Ceramic tile • Small rolling pin • Tissue blade • Plastic ruler
MATERIALS Polymer clay: scrap of brown • Gold paper: 1¼" x 1" (30mm x 25mm)

1 Roll out the brown clay on the ceramic tile, until it is about ⅛" (3mm) thick. Use the blade to cut the clay into a rectangle, ¾" x ⅜" (20mm x 10mm). Use a small rectangle of card as a template if you find it difficult to cut the clay squarely.

2 Press the edge of the ruler firmly into the clay, to score it into squares. Bake the clay on the tile for 15 minutes. When cool, wrap it in the gold paper to crease it, unwrap again and break off a few chunks if you wish.

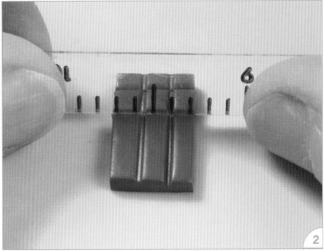

MORE IDEAS

Lollipops: Roll a sheet of beige clay, ¹/₃₂" (1mm) thick and bake for 10 minutes. Cut off strips, ¾" (20mm) long, for the lollipop sticks. Tint translucent clay with crimson, and form into ⅛" (3mm) balls. Press a ball on one end of each stick. Bake for 15 minutes. Varnish when cool.

Candy canes: Form logs of crimson and white clays, ¹/₃₂" (1mm) thick. Press these together and twist to form a candy cane. Trim to ½" (13mm) long and curve one end into a hook. Bake for 15 minutes.

Caramel apples

Caramel apples are always a favorite, particularly at Halloween. These miniature caramel apples look equally delicious—tinted varnish is used to imitate the sticky caramel coating.

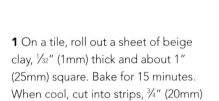

 10 minutes

TOOLS Ceramic tile • Small rolling pin • Craft knife • Paintbrush
MATERIALS Polymer clay: scraps of translucent, beige and green • Acrylic gloss varnish • Acrylic paint: brown

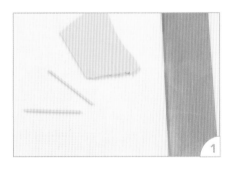

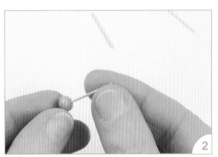

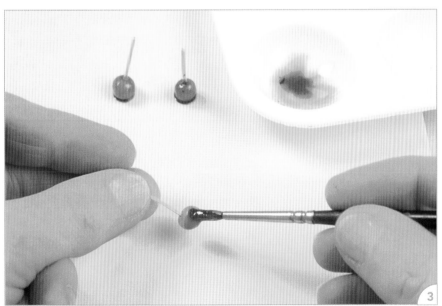

1 On a tile, roll out a sheet of beige clay, ¹⁄₃₂" (1mm) thick and about 1" (25mm) square. Bake for 15 minutes. When cool, cut into strips, ¾" (20mm) long and ¹⁄₃₂" (1mm) thick, for the sticks.

2 Tint the translucent clay with green to make a pale apple green. Make the apples from ¼" (6mm) balls, and push a stick into each one. Bake for 15 minutes.

3 When cool, mix a little brown paint into the gloss varnish to tint it. Brush liberally over the apples and stand them upright on the tile to allow a small pool to form at the base of each. Leave to dry, then apply another coat if necessary. When completely dry, slide a blade under each apple to remove it from the tile.

MORE IDEAS
Make some miniature red apples (see page 57), then follow the above instructions to make red caramel apples.

> **TIP**
> *Always make and bake miniatures on a tile. This avoids moving tiny pieces of clay, which can distort easily.*

Dollhouse pets

Dog

Every dollshouse needs pets. Miniature animals are very satisfying to model and also make delightful ornaments or collectibles for animal lovers. This soulful pup is made from gold clay.

 20 minutes

TOOLS Craft knife • Ceramic tile • Tapestry needle • Pointed tool • Brush protector
MATERIALS Polymer clay, 2oz (65g) blocks: ¼ block gold, small scraps of black
• Gloss varnish

1 To make the paws, form two ¼" (6mm) balls of gold clay, and shape each into a short log with rounded ends. Press on the tile, side by side. To make the body, form a ¾" (20mm) ball of gold, shape it into an oval, and press it on the legs (so that they protrude). Mark claws on the paws with a knife and a curve for the haunch with the needle.

2 Form a ½" (13mm) ball of brown for the head, and pinch one end into a snout. Press the head on the body. Make two eye sockets with the pointed tool and fill each with a small ball of black clay. To make the ears, form two ⅛" (3mm) balls of clay. Shape into ovals, flatten into little pancakes, press on top of the head and flap over.

3 Apply a tiny ball of black to the snout for the nose. Use the brush protector to mark two curves for lips. To make the tail, form a log 1" (25mm) long and about ⅛" (3mm) thick, making it pointed at one end. Press this on the body, curving it round to the front. Bake the dog for 20 minutes. When cool, varnish the eyes.

MORE IDEAS
Use another color of clay to reflect a different colored coat. Vary the shape of the ears, snout and tail to make a completely different breed.

> **TIP**
> *If you have a round cutter, use it to indent the curve of the dog's haunches—it will look neater than marking with a needle tool.*

Cat

This adorable little cat would look perfect sitting on a miniature rug by the fireplace. A textured gray clay has been used to suggest fur but plain gray, or any color you wish, could be used instead.

 20 minutes

TOOLS Craft knife • Ceramic tile • Tapestry needle • Pointed tool
MATERIALS Polymer clay, 2oz (65g) blocks: ¼ block textured gray (such as black Sculpey III Granitex), small scraps of golden yellow, black and white

1 Form a ½" (13mm) ball of gray clay, and shape it into a teardrop. Press it on the tile, pointed end upwards, and flatten one side a little for the front of the cat. Mark the forelegs and the curve of the back haunches. To make paws, form two ⅛" (3mm) ovals of white clay, and press one on each leg. Mark claws.

2 For the head, press a ⅜" (10mm) ball of gray on the body. Apply a ⅛" (3mm) ball of white for the muzzle. Make the nose from a tiny ball of black. Create two eye sockets with the pointed tool and fill with a ball of yellow. For the pupil, appliqué a thin, vertical strip of black on each eye (see page 25).

3 Make a small hole at the corners of the eyes to give a slanted effect. To make the ears, form two ⅛" (3mm) balls of gray, and shape into cones. Press on the head and indent at bottom center with the tapestry needle. Make the tail from a log of gray, 1" (25mm) long and pointed at one end. Bake the cat on the tile for 20 minutes.

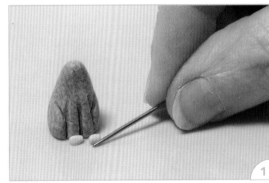

MORE IDEAS

To make a stripy ginger cat, marble together textured orange clay and white clay until streaky. Position the stripes with care. Use pale green for the eyes. To make a black cat, use black clay except for the paws, muzzle and chest, which are made of white clay. Press on the chest before applying the head.

TIP

When applying cats' ears, push the tapestry needle into the center of the ear to make the ear hole and press the ear down at the same time. This will attach the ear to the head more firmly.

Dollhouse accessories

Flowers

Making miniature flowers can be time-consuming, but this project uses tiny cutters to stamp out the flowers and leaves. Artificial stamens are available from cake decorating suppliers or craft stores.

🕐 30 minutes

TOOLS Flower cutter: ³⁄₁₆" (5mm) • Teardrop cutter: ³⁄₁₆" (5mm) • Scissors • Ceramic tile
MATERIALS Polymer clay: scraps of translucent, various colors and leaf green • Talcum powder • Artificial stamens in assorted colors • PVA glue • Fine green florist's wire, cut into several 1" (25mm) lengths

1 Use small quantities of colored clay to tint the translucent clay and make pale pastel colors. Roll these into sheets, ¹⁄₃₂" (1mm) thick. Smear the surface of the sheets with talcum powder to prevent the cutter sticking, then use the flower cutter to cut out lots of little flowers.

2 Cut each pair of stamens in half. Take one stamen, put a dab of glue on the head and thread the end through the center of a flower. Pull the flower right up to the head of the stamen, until the petals cup around it. Repeat for the other flowers.

3 Coat each length of wire (leaf stalk) with a thin layer of glue and place on the tile. Use the teardrop cutter to cut out lots of tiny leaves from thinly rolled leaf green clay, as for the flowers. Press the leaves on the stalks. Bake the flowers and leaves for 20 minutes. When cool, slide a knife blade under the stalks to free them from the tile.

MORE IDEAS
To make a flowerpot, form a basic pot shape in red-brown clay and press a disc of dark brown on top for soil. Wrap a strip of red-brown clay around the top of the flowerpot to make a lip. Make holes in the soil with a needle. Bake. Glue the flower and leaf stems in the holes.

TIP
If you cannot find artificial stamens, make your own by tying knots at 1" (25mm) intervals along a piece of strong thread. Cut the thread just above each knot and coat with glue to stiffen it.

Bag

Polymer clay simulates leather very successfully. Use it to make tiny bags or shoes—accessories that every female dollhouse occupant can never have enough of, so have fun creating the latest fashions.

 10 minutes

TOOLS Pasta machine or roller • Craft knife • Tissue blade • Tapestry needle
MATERIALS Polymer clay, 2oz (65g) blocks: ⅛ block crimson, small piece of pearl

1 Roll out a sheet of clay, about ¹⁄₁₆″ (1.5mm) thick. Cut a rectangle, 1″ (25mm) wide and 2″ (50mm) long. Trim off the top corners at an angle. Roll out a small sheet of clay, ⅛″ (3mm) thick, and cut two strips, ⅝″ (15mm) long and about ⅛″ (3mm) wide. Lay these on the long sides of the rectangle, ¾″ (20mm) from the bottom edge.

2 Fold the bottom of the rectangle up and over the strips, pressing down lightly at the sides. Roll out a sheet of clay, ¹⁄₃₂″ (1mm) thick, and cut out a strip, ⅛″ (3mm) wide and 3″ (8cm) long. Press the ends on the bag, just above the folded edge.

3 To make the bag's flap, fold the top of the rectangle over the the lower part of the bag, trapping the straps. Apply a small ball of pearl clay to the center front of the flap to make a catch. Place the bag on a tile covered with baking parchment, arranging the strap in a natural way. Bake for 20 minutes.

MORE IDEAS
Use this basic method to make bags in all shapes and sizes. Manufacture shoes by cutting soles out of sheets of clay and pressing a simple, curved strip of clay on top for the upper.

TIP
Firm (or leached, see page 17) clay will make this project much easier.

Checkers (draughts) set (page 66)

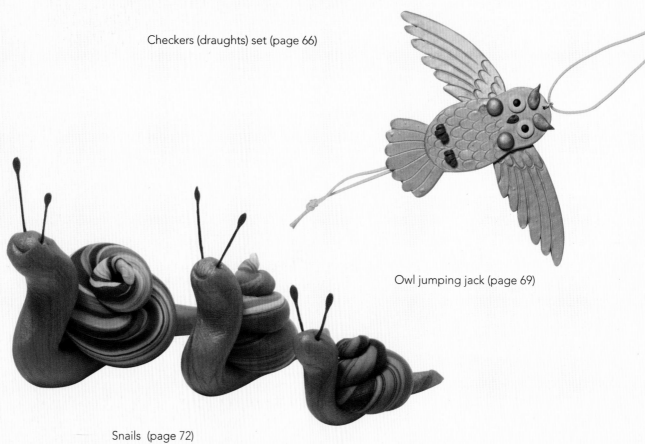

Owl jumping jack (page 69)

Snails (page 72)

CHAPTER 5
Toys and games

Top: Finger puppet
(page 68)

Bottom: Car
(page 75)

Games

Checkers (draughts) set

Quick and easy to make, this bright little checkers set with distinctive, star-shaped checkers, is much more fun to play with than a conventional checkerboard.

 1 hour

TOOLS Pasta machine or roller • Ceramic tiles • Needle • Tissue blade or knife with a long straight blade • Metal ruler • Heavy-duty craft knife • Star cutter: ½" (13mm)

MATERIALS Polymer clay, 2oz (65g) blocks: 1 block translucent, 1 block light blue, ½ block magenta, ½ block yellow • Graph paper • PVA glue • Talcum powder • Thick cardboard: 6.5" (16.5cm) square

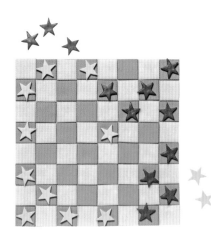

1 To make the checkerboard squares, roll out the light blue clay on a tile, ¹⁄₁₆" (1.5mm) thick. Place the graph paper on top and prick through at ¾" (2cm) intervals to transfer the grid to the clay. Cut along the lines to make 32 squares measuring ¾" (2cm) square. Remove the waste clay from the edges. Repeat for the translucent clay.

2 Bake the squares (on the ceramic tiles) for 20 minutes. Remove when cool and glue to the cardboard in rows of eight, alternating the colors. Leave to dry and then if necessary, trim the edges of the cardboard using a metal ruler and a sharp knife.

3 To make the checkers, roll the magenta clay into a sheet ¹⁄₁₆" (1.5mm) thick. Lightly dust the surface with talcum powder and cut out twelve stars. Repeat with the yellow clay to make the yellow stars. Bake the stars for 20 minutes.

MORE IDEAS
Experiment by using different shaped cutters for the pieces. There are many to choose from, such as flowers or hearts. You could also design an even brighter color scheme, and use slices from a millefiori cane to decorate the pieces.

TIP
To cut the squares quickly, use a large carving knife with a straight blade.

66 TOYS AND GAMES

Dominoes

Playing dominoes is especially enjoyable when you have made the domino set yourself. This project uses a texture plate for the backs of the dominoes but textured paper, lace or fabric can be used instead.

 1¼ hours

TOOLS Pasta machine or roller • Ceramic tiles • Needle • Tissue blade or knife with a long, straight blade • Ball tool or the blunt end of a paintbrush handle, ³⁄₁₆" (5mm) in diameter • Plastic texture plate, any size

MATERIALS Polymer clay, 2oz (65g) blocks: 3 blocks black • Graph paper: standard letter size (A4) • Talcum powder • Pearlescent or metallic powder in six different colors • PVA glue • Gloss varnish

1 Draw lines on the graph paper to divide it into rectangles measuring ¾" x 1½" (2cm x 4cm). Roll out a sheet of black clay on a tile, making it as large as will fit on the tile and ¹⁄₁₂" (2mm) thick. Put the graph paper on the clay and prick the corners of the rectangles to mark the clay below. Cut out the rectangles and lightly mark the center line across each domino with the edge of a ruler. You will need 28 rectangles so repeat as necessary on another tile.

2 Remove waste clay from around the rectangles. Dip the ball tool into the powder color, shake off the excess, and use this to mark domino spots (change the powder color for different numbers). Use the photographs as a guide to placing the spots. Make one domino for each combination of numbers from one to six, plus a blank domino—28 in total.

3 To make textured backs for the dominoes, roll out a second sheet of black clay, as in Step 1, and dust the surface with talc. Place the texture sheet on it and roll it through the pasta machine on the same setting (or roll over it firmly with your roller). Peel back the sheet to reveal the texture and brush on metallic powder with your fingertip. Now cut out 28 rectangles as before. Bake all the pieces for 30 minutes. When the pieces are cool, glue the backs to the dominoes and varnish the spots to protect them.

MORE IDEAS
Try making dominoes in bright colors. The indented spots can be filled with colored liquid polymer clay instead of pearlescent or metallic powder.

TIP
Use a large tapestry needle to mark holes on the textured clay through the graph paper, otherwise the pricks will be hard to see.

Playthings

Finger puppet

Finger puppets make perfect bedtime storytelling aids. This project shows you how to make a cowboy, but the instructions can easily be adapted to make many other characters—in no time at all you can create a diverse cast of mini folk.

 30 minutes   Template: see page 106

TOOLS Former: shape scrap clay into a log the same size as your finger, trim to 1¼" (4cm) long and bake for 20 minutes • Pasta machine or roller • Craft knife • Brush protector
MATERIALS Polymer clay: small quantities of flesh, turquoise, brown, gold, red and black
• Aluminum foil

1 Wrap the former tightly in aluminum foil. Roll out a sheet of flesh clay, ⅟₁₆" (1.5mm) thick, and use this to cover the top ¾" (20mm) of the former. Smooth the joins and trim the bottom edge. Roll a sheet of turquoise clay of the same thickness and use it to cover the bottom of the former loosely, butting the top edge against the flesh clay. Pull out the bottom edge a little all around, so the former will be easy to remove later.

2 Roll out small sheets of gold, red and brown clay and use the templates to cut out the hair, neckerchief and hat brim. Fringe the edges of the hair and press on the head. Form a ⅝" (15mm) ball of brown clay for the hat crown, flatten the bottom and indént the top, then press it on the hat brim. Press the hat on the head.

3 To make the eyes, apply two tiny balls of black, and use a small ball of flesh for the nose. Indent a smiling mouth. Wrap the long piece of the neckerchief around the neck and press on the two tail pieces. Apply a ball of red for the knot. Bake the puppet for 30 minutes. While it is still warm, gently ease it off the form.

MORE IDEAS
Use the basic pattern to make lots of finger puppets, such as the Native American girl pictured. Other ideas are a soldier, sailor, gypsy, princess, clown, ghost, firefighter or police officer.

TIP
If it is difficult to remove the puppet from the former, make a cut up the puppet's back with the knife. Take the puppet off the former and then glue the sides of the cut together again.

Owl jumping jack

Originating in the nineteenth century, a jumping jack is a figure made in card or wood that waves its arms and legs when a cord at the back is pulled. This polymer clay version features an owl that flaps its wings instead.

 1 hour　　　　　　　　　　Template: see page 107

TOOLS Pasta machine or roller • Templates, traced and cut out • Ceramic tile • Craft knife • Brush protector or round cutter: ⅛" (3mm) • Tapestry needle • Darning needle • Wire cutters
MATERIALS Polymer clay, 2oz (65g) blocks: 1 block gold, scraps of black, brown and beige • Strong thread • 2 paper fasteners • Jump ring: ⅛" (3mm) in diameter • Golden yellow cord: two lengths, 12" (30cm) long and ¹⁄₁₆" (1.5mm) thick

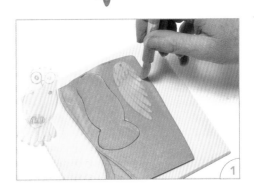

1 Roll out the gold clay into a sheet, fold in half and roll again several times until all streaks have disappeared. Finally, roll into a sheet ¹⁄₁₆" (1.5mm) thick and place on the tile. Cut out the pieces using the traced templates, remove the waste clay and leave the pieces on the tile.

2 Mark feathers on the owl, using the template as a guide. Use the cutter or brush protector to make ⅛" (3mm) holes in the body and wings where indicated on the templates. Make smaller holes in the tops of the wings for the thread. Cover the heads of the paper fasteners with gold clay.

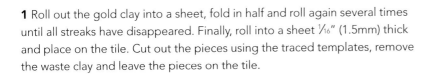

3 To make the eyes, press two ¼" (6mm) balls of beige clay on the face, and apply two smaller balls of black for the pupils. Apply a small teardrop of brown for the beak and mark nostrils. For the ears, shape two ¼" (6mm) balls of gold into teardrops. For the feet, form two ¼" (6mm) balls of brown into teardrops, and flatten on the tile. Cut toes, shape into a curl and press on the body.

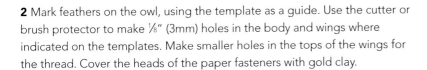

4 Bake all the pieces for 30 minutes. Assemble the owl with the paper fasteners pushed through the large holes in the wings and body. Trim the ends of the fasteners with the wire cutters. Tie thread loosely between the small wing holes, and attach one of the cords to the thread. Pull the cord and the wings should lift. Attach the jump ring to the head hole and tie on the other cord to suspend the owl.

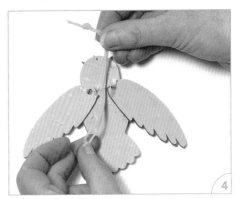

TIP
The paper fasteners need to be attached loosely so that the wings will flap freely.

Pocket doll

This tiny doll has enormous appeal for young and old alike. It is jointed and can be made to sit or stand. You can decorate the dress by gluing scraps of narrow lace or ribbon around the bottom edge.

 1½ hours   Template: see page 107

TOOLS Craft knife • Darning needle • Fine paintbrush • Template for dress, traced and cut out • Needle

MATERIALS Polymer clay, 2oz (65g) blocks: ¼ block flesh, small scrap of black • Wire (22 gauge): 1" (25mm) long • Thread elastic: 6" (15cm) long and approximately ¹⁄₃₂" (1mm) wide • Rubbing alcohol (methylated spirits) • Acrylic paint: red, black, white and blue • Small piece of fabric in a tiny print • Thread • Fabric glue • Embroidery silk: pale yellow

1 Body: form a ½" (13mm) ball of flesh clay into an oval. Flatten it slightly and pinch the bottom into a point. Neck: push the wire into the body and thread on a log of flesh clay, ⅛" (3mm) long and the same thickness. Head: push a ½" (13mm) ball of flesh on the end of the wire.

2 Limbs: form a log of flesh clay, ⅛" (3mm) thick, and cut four lengths of ¾" (20mm). Arms: round one end of a length, flatten it and cut out a V-shaped notch to make the hand (reverse the V for the other arm). Feet: form two ³⁄₁₆" (5mm) ovals of black clay, and press on the legs.

3 Pinch the tops of the arms and legs to flatten them slightly and arrange against the body. Pierce a hole right through the tops of the arms and upper body. Repeat for the legs. Bake all the pieces for 30 minutes. When they are cool, tie a knot in a length of elastic and thread the end through one arm, the upper body and the other arm. Tie a knot in the other end and use the needle to pull it down tightly on to the arm. Attach the legs in the same way.

4 Brush the face with rubbing alcohol (methylated spirits) and paint on features. Cut out the dress pieces. Run a gathering thread along one long end of the skirt and pull it around the doll, stitching it to secure it around the chest. Glue the bodice over the top of the skirt, covering the raw edges. For hair, glue on lengths of embroidery thread, bound in the center.

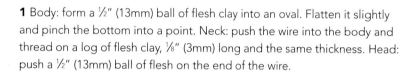

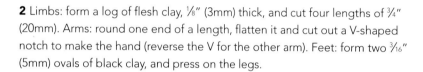

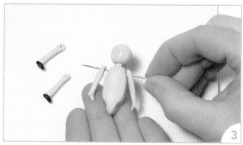

TIP
See Stringing a Necklace (page 33) for how to pull the knot in the elastic tightly when attaching the arms and legs to the body.

Toy flute

This flute can actually be played! Make sure that the mouth hole is cut cleanly in order to achieve the best sound. Hold the flute horizontally and blow across the mouth hole to make a haunting note.

 45 minutes

TOOLS Pasta machine or roller • Length of smooth plant stake (garden cane): ½" (13mm) in diameter and about 12" (30cm) long • Craft knife • Tissue blade • Cookie sheet (baking sheet) covered with baking parchment • Brush protectors or circle cutters: ¼" (6mm) and ³⁄₁₆" (5mm)
MATERIALS Polymer clay, 2oz (65g) blocks: 1 block pearl green • Aluminum foil • Tape • Superglue

1 Wrap the plant stake tightly in foil and secure with tape. Roll out a sheet of clay, ¹⁄₁₂" (2mm) thick, 10" (25cm) long and about 3" (75mm) wide. Wrap this around the foil-covered plant stake. Trim the edges so that they butt together, with no overlap, and smooth the join. Trim each end of the flute by rolling it against the blade. The flute should be about 9½" (24cm) long.

2 Use the ¼" (6mm) brush protector to make a mouth hole 1" (25mm) from one end. Use the ³⁄₁₆" (5mm) brush protector to make a finger hole, 1⅜" (35mm) from the other end. Cut four more finger holes at 1" (25mm) intervals along the flute. If the cut pieces will not come out, leave them to be removed after baking.

3 Form a ½" (13mm) ball of clay, and press flat to make a disc wide enough to cover the end of the flute. Bake the flute (on the plant stake) and disc for 30 minutes. While the flute is still warm, slide it carefully off the plant stake and pull the foil away. Glue the disc to the end nearest the mouth hole.

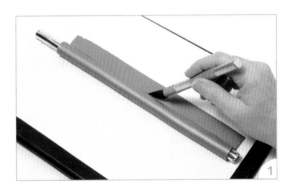

MORE IDEAS
Use a dark clay and stamp it with a small stamp before baking. Apply gold powder sparingly to suggest weathered bronze. Alternatively, try decorating a flute with grooves made with a knitting needle before baking (see page 20).

Models

Snails

These snail models make delightful gifts for people of all ages. For variety you can try making them in ever-decreasing sizes and in a whole rainbow of colors.

TOOLS Ceramic tile • Craft knife • Needle • Brush protector
MATERIALS Polymer clay, 2oz (65g) blocks: ¼ block gold, scraps of various colors for the shells • Artificial stamens or fine wire

1 To make the body, form a ⅝" (15mm) ball of gold clay, and roll it into a tapered log, 2⅜" (6cm) long. Point the thin end to make the tail. Press the body on the tile, making a wiggle in the end of the tail.

2 To make the shell, form three ½" (13mm) balls of clay, each a different color. Roll these into logs, 2" (5cm) long. Marble the logs together (see page 24) until the colors are in colorful streaks. Shape into one tapered log, 3" (7.5cm) long. Twist the log along its length and coil clockwise into a snail shell, with the tapered end at the top.

3 Press the shell onto the center of the body and push the head end up to meet the shell. Pierce two eyeholes with the needle and insert a stamen in each for the feelers. (Fine wire can be used instead.) Mark a smiling mouth with the brush protector. Bake the snail for 20 minutes.

MORE IDEAS
Make snails in lots of different sizes. Experiment with the colors in the marbling to make beautiful and unusual color combinations.

TIP
The eye of a large needle, held upside down, will mark a minute mouth on the tiniest of snails.

House

It is not difficult to make this diminutive house. Sheets of polymer clay are cut according to the pattern, baked and then assembled. Make a whole neighborhood of houses by varying the colors and embellishments.

 1 hour   Template: see page 108

TOOLS Pasta machine or roller • Template, traced and cut out • Ceramic tiles • Craft knife • Tissue blade • Ruler • Tapestry needle
MATERIALS Polymer clay, 2oz (65g) blocks: ½ block white, ¼ block copper, small quantities of black and light blue • Superglue

1 Walls: roll out a sheet of white clay, ¹⁄₁₆" (1.5mm) thick, on the tile. Use the templates to cut out the walls and base, removing waste clay from around them and leaving them on the tile to bake. Roof: make the pieces from copper clay in the same way. Mark horizontal lines of tiles with the edge of the ruler, and vertical lines with the tapestry needle.

2 Chimney: cut a slice of white clay, ¼" (6mm) thick, straight from the block. Cut out the shape with the template. Press a tiny log of copper on top for a chimney pot. Windows and shutters: roll out sheets of black and light blue clay, ¹⁄₃₂" (1mm) thick. Cut four ¼" (6mm) squares of black for the windows and mark with diagonal lines to simulate panes of glass. Cut blue shutters and press to the windows. Mark horizontal lines on the shutters. Apply thin strips of blue to the top and bottom of the windows.

3 Door: cut from the light blue sheet, mark vertical lines and apply a tiny ball for a doorknob. Bake all the pieces on the tiles for 30 minutes. Glue the walls together and glue the windows and door to the house front. Glue the roof and chimney in position.

MORE IDEAS
Make a smaller house by cutting a narrower template for the house front, back, roof and base. Try making houses with walls, roofs and windows in a different color. You could appliqué a rambling rose up the house front (see the Windmill project on page 86).

> ### TIP
> *Cut the house pieces as accurately as possible so they fit well on assembly. After baking trim the edges with a knife, if necessary.*

Car

I love making models that work and this little car will happily roll along on its cocktail stick axles and polymer clay wheels.

 1½ hours

TOOLS Pasta machine or roller • Ceramic tile • Craft knife • Tissue blade • Pen cap • Tapestry needle
MATERIALS Polymer clay, 2oz (65g) blocks: ½ block blue, ¼ block black, scraps of white and gold • Liquid polymer clay • 2 cocktail sticks • Bamboo barbecue skewer (needs to be thicker than the cocktail sticks) cut into two 2" (5cm) lengths • Superglue • Silver acrylic paint • Gloss varnish

1 Chassis: roll out a sheet of black clay, ¹⁄₁₆" (1.5mm) thick, and cut out a rectangle, 1½" x ¾" (4cm x 2cm). Put this on the tile and place the skewer pieces across it, about ⅜" (1cm) from each end. Cut four strips of clay from the remaining sheet and lay these over the skewers, pressing them down well on either side. Bake on the tile for 30 minutes. Remove the skewers.

2 Wheels: form four ⁵⁄₁₆" (8mm) balls of black clay, and press each down on the tile to make a disc, ½" (13mm) in diameter. Stamp with the end of a pen cap to suggest a hubcap. Make a hole in the center with the tapestry needle, large enough to take the cocktail stick.

3 Brush liquid clay thinly over the top of the baked chassis. Seats: flatten four ⅛" (3mm) ovals of gold clay, and mark with vertical lines. Hood (bonnet) and trunk (boot): form a log of blue clay, ⅝" (15mm) thick and 1⅜" (35mm) long, with rounded ends. Cut into two, ½" (13mm) from one end. Press the hood (bonnet—the longer piece) on the chassis at the front. Apply the trunk (boot) to the rear of the chassis. Position the seats in the gap.

> **TIP**
> *To make the car run evenly, take care to make the car's wheels absolutely round and place the axle holes in the exact center of each wheel.*

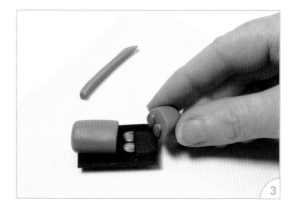

4 Hood (bonnet) trim: apply a strip of blue clay over the car front. Wheel arches: form four ⅜" (10mm) balls of blue clay, and shape them into rounded logs, 1" (25mm) long. Press on the sides of the car, curving into place. Make sure that they are high enough to allow the wheels to turn freely.

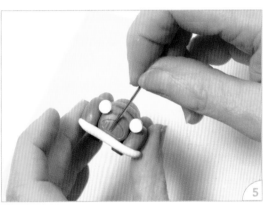

5 Headlights: form a ⅜" (10mm) ball of white clay, elongate it slightly, cut in half and press on either side of the hood (bonnet). Bumpers: form two logs of white, ⅛" (3mm) wide and 1¼" (30mm) long, point the ends and press on the car. Mark lines on the front of the hood to simulate a radiator grille.

6 Replace the skewers and bake both the model and the wheels for 30 minutes. Remove the skewers. Cut the cocktail sticks so that they are ¼" (6mm) longer than the width of the chassis. Glue one end into the hole in a wheel, push the other end through the axle holes and then glue on the other wheel. Check that the axles turn freely, trimming away excess clay under the wheel arches if necessary.

7 Paint the bumpers, radiator, headlights and wheel centers with silver paint. Varnish the blue clay to give the paintwork a shiny look.

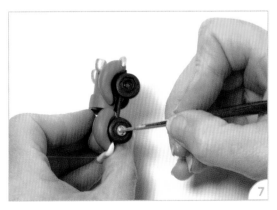

MORE IDEAS

This car can be made in any color you like—even two-tone. Try adding more details such as a small disc of clay for a steering wheel, or license plates.

Snow scene nightlight (page 88)

Flowery frame (page 84)

Seagull pen holder (page 79)

CHAPTER 6
Accessories for the home

Top: Hen and chicks eggcup (page 81)

Bottom: Clary the cow fridge magnet (page 87)

Desk accessories

Bookworm bookmark

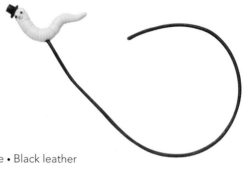

This jolly little wriggler marks your page and looks as though it is undulating along the top of the book. It is quick and easy to make and perfect for a small gift.

 20 minutes

TOOLS Ceramic tile • Craft knife • Brush protector • Tapestry needle
MATERIALS Polymer clay: ½" (13mm) ball of pale green clay, scraps of black and white • Black leather thong, ¹⁄₃₂" (1mm) thick and about 12" (30cm) long • Superglue

1 Shape the ball of pale green clay into a tapered log, about 2" (5cm) long. Mark worm-like wrinkles on the sides with the back of your knife. Curve the worm into a wiggly shape and press down lightly on the tile.

2 Mark a mouth with the brush protector. To make the eyes, form two ¹⁄₁₆" (1.5mm) balls of white clay, and press on the head. Form two slightly smaller balls of black clay to make the pupils. Use a small ball of pale green for the nose.

3 To make the hat, flatten a ⅛" (3mm) ball of black clay, and press on the head to make the brim. Cut a ⅛" (3mm) length from a log of the same thickness for the crown and press on top of the brim. Make a hole in the bottom of the worm for the thong. Bake the worm on the tile for 20 minutes. When cool, glue the end of the thong into the hole.

MORE IDEAS
Vary the colors of the body, hat and thong. Experiment with a range of hats, from a peaked cap to a beanie hat or even a stetson.

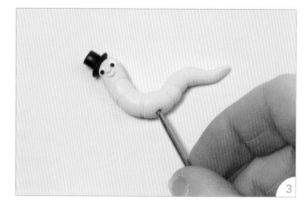

TIP
When mixing pastel colors, you usually need a lot more white clay than colored clay. The exact quantities will depend on the brand of clay.

Seagull pen holder

This unusual pen holder—a perky seagull perched on polymer clay rocks that grip a ballpoint pen—will brighten up your desktop. Granite-effect clay gives the rocks a realistic texture.

 1 hour

TOOLS Craft knife • Ceramic tile • Ballpoint pen • Tapestry needle
MATERIALS Polymer clay, 2oz (65g) blocks: 1 block of black granite-effect clay (or any gray or stone-effect clay), ¼ block of blue granite-effect clay, small amounts of white, golden yellow and black • Gilt wire (20–22 gauge): 2" (5cm)

NB: For best results, do not knead the granite- or stone-effect clays.

1 Use black granite clay roughly to shape three rocks as pictured. Make pebbles from black and blue granite clays. Press all the stones in position. Remove the pen cap and push the pen well into the large rock to make a hole of the correct size.

2 To make the seagull's feet, form two ⅛" (3mm) balls of yellow into cones. Press them flat on the tile, making two small triangles, and use the tapestry needle to mark toes. Position the feet on the highest rock. For the legs, cut the wire in two and push each length about ¼" (6mm) into the rock.

3 For the gull's body, form a ½" (13mm) ball of white clay, and shape it into a teardrop. Mark wing feathers with the eye of the needle. Make the head from a ¼" (6mm) ball of white. Indent eye sockets and fill with tiny balls of black. Make a beak from a cone of yellow.

4 Press the gull's body onto the legs, pushing it down well to secure it. Bake the piece on the tile for 30 minutes. The hole in the rock will form a cap for the pen and prevent it drying out.

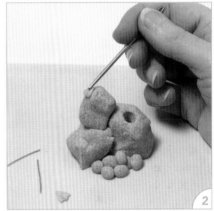

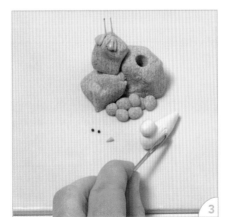

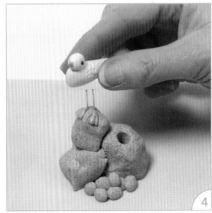

TIP
As you make the rocks, press them together firmly so that they do not come apart after baking.

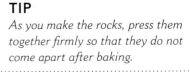

Tableware

Patchwork coasters

These sumptuous coasters are reminiscent of patchwork brocade. Several different techniques are used to give an interesting variety of textures. Scrap clay can be used up to make the backing—simply mix all the scraps together to make a neutral gray.

 30 minutes (plus drying time for the ink)

TOOLS Pasta machine or roller • Ceramic tiles • Tissue blade or straight-bladed knife • Piece of lace
MATERIALS FOR TWO COASTERS Polymer clay, 2oz (65g) blocks: ½ block black, ½ block dark blue, 1 block gray (or use scrap clay)
• Pearlescent inks: turquoise, lilac • Pearlescent powders: a variety (bronze, yellow-green and silver have been used here)
• Graph paper • Gloss varnish

1 Crackle clay: roll out some black clay to about ⅛" (3mm) thick and coat the surface generously with alternating stripes of the pearlescent inks. Leave to dry for an hour or more until the surface is completely dry. Now roll the sheet firmly until it is 1⁄16" (1.5mm) thick (or pass through a pasta machine). This will make the dried ink crackle. Repeat with blue clay for a different color effect.

2 Lace clay: roll out a sheet of black clay, 1⁄16" (1.5mm) thick. Place the lace on top and roll again firmly (or pass through the pasta machine on the same setting as before). Peel off the lace. Dip your finger into pearlescent powder and stroke it over the surface of the clay to highlight the raised areas. Repeat with blue clay.

3 Make ¾" (20mm) squares of mosaic from the textured clay (see page 66) and bake for 20 minutes. You will need 16 assorted squares for each coaster. Roll out a sheet of gray clay, 1⁄16" (1.5mm) thick, and press the squares onto it, alternating colors and textures. Trim around the coasters and bake on the tile for 30 minutes. Varnish to protect the surface.

MORE IDEAS
Try using different colors of clay and ink to create other color schemes. Strongly textured fabric such as burlap (hessian) or brocade can be used instead of the lace.

> **TIP**
> *If you roll the inked clay in two different directions instead of just one, you will get a more shattered crackle effect. However, do not roll the surface too many times or the colors will dim.*

Hen and chicks eggcup

The most natural motif for decorating an eggcup is surely a plump mother hen and her tiny yellow chicks! The clay is easily shaped into an attractive relief that is applied to a china or glass eggcup and then baked.

 30 minutes per eggcup

TOOLS • Craft knife • Tapestry needle
MATERIALS Polymer clay: small quantities of gold, copper, golden yellow, black, brown • Plain white china eggcup • Rubbing alcohol (methylated spirits)

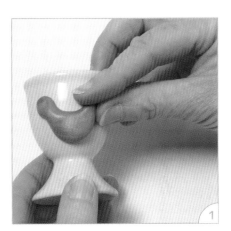

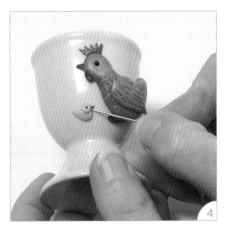

1 Wipe the eggcup with rubbing alcohol (methylated spirits) to degrease the surface. To make the hen, form a ⅝" (15mm) ball of gold clay. Shape it into an oval and roll one end between your fingers to make the neck. Pinch out the tail and then press the hen shape on the side of the eggcup until it is about ⅛" (3mm) thick.

2 To make the wing, form a ⁵⁄₁₆" (8mm) ball of gold, and shape it into a teardrop. Flatten it into a wing shape and press it on the hen. Mark feathers with the eye of the needle. To make the comb, form a log of copper, ¹⁄₁₆" (1.5mm) thick, flatten and trim to ¼" (6mm) long. Cut wedges from the top. Press on top of the head.

3 Apply a small cone of brown for the beak and a small oval of copper below it for the wattle. Make an eye socket with the needle and press in a tiny black ball for the eye. Make a foot from an oval of copper clay and press in place.

4 For the chicks, use a tiny teardrop of yellow clay for the body, and a small ball for the head. Apply a tiny cone of copper for the beak and a black ball for the eye. Bake the eggcup for 30 minutes. When cool, check that the applied clay is firmly fixed to the china and if not, re-apply using Superglue. The eggcups should be handwashed.

TIP

To give a lovely sheen to the hen's feathers, use gold clay containing mica. It should be rolled into a sheet, folded in half and rolled again several times to produce maximum sheen and eliminate streaks.

Ornaments

Millefiori egg

Applying slices of millefiori cane to blown hens' eggs has always been a popular project with polymer clay enthusiasts and this version is particularly quick and easy. Any of your favorite canes can be used for this technique. The eggs look very stylish displayed in an attractive bowl or basket.

 1 hour

TOOLS Tapestry needle • Bowl •Tissue blade • Soft brush • Small roller or pen barrel
MATERIALS Polymer clay: millefiori flower cane (see page 31) and leaf cane (see page 29) • Hen's egg • Talcum powder • Fine sandpaper • Quilt batting (wadding)

1 Make a small hole in each end of the egg. Hold it over a bowl and blow hard into one hole to expel the contents through the other hole. Rinse well and place in a low oven for 20 minutes to dry.

2 Reduce the diameter of the canes: the flower cane to ½" (13mm) and the leaf cane to about ⅜" (10mm). Cut even slices from the canes, about $\frac{1}{32}$" (1mm) thick. Apply them to the egg, placing an occasional leaf between the flowers. Butt the slices against each other and press them on firmly, taking care not to crack the eggshell.

3 Continue until the whole of the egg is covered, leaving a small gap over the holes in the shell to allow air to expand during baking. Dust the surface with talcum powder and roll over the slices with a roller to further flatten them and press them together. Bake the egg on baking parchment for 30 minutes. If a very smooth finish is desired, sand and buff the egg with quilt batting (wadding), but this takes a lot more time (see page 27).

MORE IDEAS
This technique can also be used to cover a large smooth pebble with millefiori slices to make a paperweight.

TIP
Try to cut all the slices exactly the same thickness—this will give the egg a much smoother finish.

Leaf mobile

Translucent clay is ideal for projects where light will shine through the clay, and this mobile looks wonderful hung in a window. Use a strong polymer clay (such as Premo Sculpey or Fimo Classic) so that the leaves can be made paper-thin without breaking. Leaf colors have been chosen to reflect autumn colors.

 1 hour   Template: see page 108

TOOLS • Pasta machine or roller • Leaf templates, traced and cut out • Craft knife • Tapestry needle • Tissue blade

MATERIALS Polymer clay, 2oz (65g) blocks: 1 block translucent; ½ block beige, scraps of orange, yellow, crimson • Aluminum foil • 2 bamboo barbecue skewers • Strong thread

MIXTURES To make translucent yellow: ¼ block translucent clay, tiny quantity of yellow. To make translucent orange: ¼ block translucent clay, tiny quantity of orange. To make translucent red: ¼ block translucent clay, tiny quantity of red. (See page 00.)

1 Marble the three different translucent colors together lightly to make broad bands of color (see page 24). Roll into a thin sheet, ¹⁄₃₂" (1mm) thick or less. Press the sheet down lightly on a smooth workboard and use the templates to cut out the leaves—five large and three small.

2 Mark veins on each leaf with the tapestry needle and make a hole in the stem end for hanging. Slide the tissue blade under the leaf to free it from the surface and pinch along the veins from beneath the leaf to curve it into a natural shape. Place it on a piece of foil curved to support it while it bakes. Repeat for the remaining leaves.

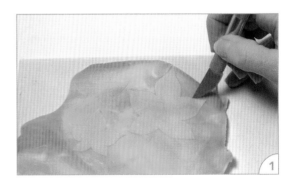

3 To make the holder for the arms of the mobile, form a log of beige clay, ½" (13mm) thick. Trim it to 2" (5cm) long, flatten one end and pierce a hole to hang it with. Make two holes below it, at right angles to each other, to take the skewers. Bake all the pieces for 30 minutes.

4 Trim the skewers to 9" (23cm) long and push one into each skewer hole. Tie a thread to the hanging hole and hang the mobile up. Attach four leaves to each skewer with thread of varying lengths, so that they form a pretty shower, spacing them equally.

> ## TIP
> *Polymer clay tends to cockle when rolled into very thin sheets, but in this project the effect will make the leaves more realistic.*

Picture frames

Flowery frame

Make a simple glass frame stand out from the crowd by decorating it with dainty flowers. The flowers are quick and easy to make using cutters, but the shapes can be cut out by hand if you wish.

 30 minutes

TOOLS Pasta machine or roller • Soft brush • Flower cutters: ¾" (20mm), ½" (13mm) and ³⁄₁₆" (5mm) • Teardrop (or leaf) cutter: ⅜" (10mm) • Craft knife • Tapestry needle
MATERIALS Polymer Clay: small amounts of magenta, yellow and green • Rubbing alcohol (methylated spirits) • Talcum powder • Glass clip frame: 6" x 4" (15cm x 10cm)

1 Dismantle the frame and wipe the surface of the glass with rubbing alcohol (methylated spirits) to degrease it. Roll out a sheet of magenta clay, ¹⁄₁₆" (1.5mm) thick. Brush the surface with talcum powder to prevent sticking and cut a flower with each of the two larger flower cutters.

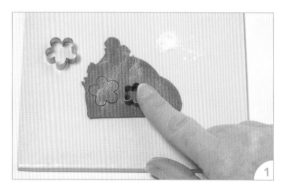

2 Press the large flower on the bottom corner of the frame and the smaller flower on the opposite top corner. Roll out the green clay to the same thickness and cut out seven leaves with the teardrop cutter. Press these around the flowers, using the photographs as a guide, and mark veins with your knife.

3 Use the tiny flower cutter to cut lots of shapes from a sheet of yellow clay of the same thickness. Press these around the large flowers and in the center of each flower. Make a hole in each yellow flower with the needle and

indent the petals of the large flowers with a paintbrush.

4 Bake the flowers on the glass for 20 minutes and leave to cool. Assemble the frame, using a paper mount in a contrasting color that shows off the flowers. The flowers should adhere to the glass well, but if any become loose, they can be glued on with Superglue.

MORE IDEAS
Frames can be decorated with all kinds of images, using the same method—try using star cutters and rainbow colors for a really lively frame.

TIP
After baking, remove any fingerprints on the glass with a cotton swab (cotton bud) dipped in rubbing alcohol (methylated spirits); take care not to dislodge the flowers.

Faux wood picture frame

Framed silhouettes were very popular in the nineteenth century and this frame is almost indistinguishable from an antique version—polymer clay makes excellent faux wood. Use silhouettes of family members to make your own heirlooms.

 1 hour   Template: see page 109

TOOLS Pasta machine or roller • 2 ceramic tiles • Mug or glass • Template traced onto stiff card and cut out

MATERIALS Polymer clay, 2oz (65g) blocks: ½ block dark brown, 1 block black, ¼ block gold • Talcum powder • Wire for hanging: 2½" (65mm) long • Silhouette to fit the frame • Small piece of thin acetate (optional)

1 Marble together ¼ block of brown, ¼ block of gold and ¼ block of black clay until the streaks are fine (see page 24). Roll the marbled clay into a sheet, about ⅛" (3mm) thick, and place it on the tile. Use the template to cut out the frame, and remove the waste clay. Dust the surface of the frame with talcum powder and use the rim of the mug to make an indentation in it, making sure that it is centered.

2 Form a log of gold clay, ⅛" (3mm) thick, and apply it to the inside of the frame opening, butting the ends together neatly. Roll out a sheet of black clay, ⅛" (3mm) thick, on the second tile. Use the template to cut out the frame back, omitting the center hole.

3 Bend the wire into a triangle for a hanging loop and secure it to the top of the frame back with a strip of clay, pressed down firmly. Bake the frame for 30 minutes. When cool, glue your chosen picture to the back of the frame front. Glue the front and back frames together. (If you want the image to be protected, glue a small piece of acetate to the back of the frame front before attaching the picture.)

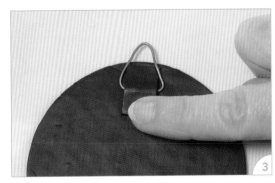

MORE IDEAS
Frames can be made in many sizes using this method. A small stamp could be used to suggest carved wood.

> **TIP**
> *Instead of the template, large round cookie cutters could be used to cut out the frames.*

Fridge magnets

Windmill fridge magnet

Windmills are beautiful old buildings and their distinctive shape makes a very attractive fridge magnet. This windmill gains additional color from the rambling roses scrambling above the door.

 30 minutes

TOOLS Pasta machine or roller • Ceramic tile • Craft knife • Tissue blade • Tapestry needle
MATERIALS Polymer clay: small quantities of dark brown, white, leaf green, black, crimson • Fridge magnet • Superglue
MIXTURES To make pale leaf green: ½" (13mm) ball of leaf green, ½" (13mm) ball of white

1 To make the sails, roll a sheet of white clay, 1/16" (1.5mm) thick. Cut a strip, 1½" (35mm) long and ¼" (6mm) wide, and press it on the tile at an angle. Cut two more strips, 5/8" (15mm) long (same width). Butt these against the first strip. On each sail, mark horizontal lines and a vertical central line.

2 To make the windmill tower, form a ball of dark brown clay into a tapered log, 5/8" (15mm) long. Press it down on the ceramic tile, trim the top and bottom and mark lines to suggest brickwork. To make the top of the windmill, cut a ½" (13mm) oval of white clay in half. Press one half on top of the tower and mark with horizontal lines. To make the wheel, press flat a 1/16" (1.5mm) ball of white, and mark it with radiating lines. Place at the top left of the windmill.

3 Press the windmill on the sails. For the grassy base, form a log of pale leaf green, ¼" (6mm) thick, and press it across the bottom of the windmill, trimming to length. Apply two tiny rectangles of black clay for windows (see page 25 Appliqué). Apply thin strips of white clay around them for the window frames, and a small rectangle of white for a door, with a tiny black ball for the doorknob.

4 For the rose, press a thin thread of leaf green on the windmill, and cut and apply leaves and flowers (see page 25). Pierce the center of each flower. Bake the windmill on the tile for 20 minutes. When it is cool, glue the magnet to the back.

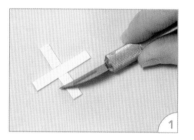

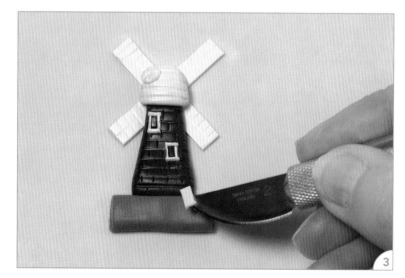

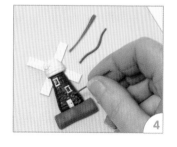

TIP
To appliqué rectangles, roll out a thin sheet and cut a strip of the required width. Cut a rectangle from this, lift it with the knife blade and apply as for normal appliqué (see page 25).

Clary the cow fridge magnet

Farm animals make entertaining fridge magnets and Clary the cow is no exception. She could also be made into an amusing brooch by gluing a brooch pin to the back instead of a magnet.

 20 minutes

TOOLS Ceramic tile • Craft knife • Tapestry needle
MATERIALS Polymer clay, 2oz (65g) blocks: ¼ block white, scraps of black, gray and light flesh • Fridge magnet • Superglue

1 To make the legs, form a log of white clay, ¼" (6mm) thick. Cut two pieces, ½" (13mm) long, and press on the tile. Mark a vertical line down the center of each to simulate four legs. For the body, form a ⅝" (15mm) ball of white, and press two ovals of black on it to make the patches. Roll the ball in your hands to smooth in the patches. Shape into an oval and press it on the legs.

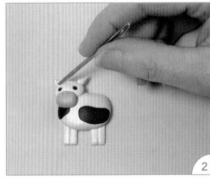

2 To make the head, form a ⅜" (10mm) ball of white into an oval. Press it on the left of the body. For the muzzle, add a ¼" (6mm) ball of light flesh. Make holes for the nostrils. Make eye sockets and fill with two tiny balls of black. Make ears by rolling two ⅛" (3mm) balls of white into teardrops. Press them on the head and mark earholes.

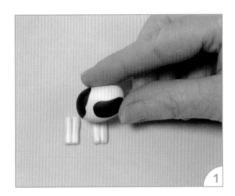

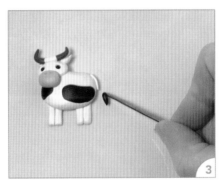

3 To make the horns, form a ¼" (6mm) ball of gray clay, roll it into a pointed log and cut in half. Assemble the horns with a white log, ¼" (6mm) long, between them. Press on the head, curving the horns upwards. For the tail, apply a thin log of white with a black oval on the end.

4 To make hoofs, appliqué thin slices from a gray log, ⅛" (3mm) thick, on the legs. Mark a cleft in the center of each. Bake the cow on the tile for 30 minutes. When cool, glue a magnet to the back.

TIP
When pressing the cow's body on its legs, make sure that the black patches are in suitable positions.

Lights

Snow scene nightlight

Liquid polymer clay creates wonderful stained glass effects, and the frosty scene on this nightlight looks beautiful when illuminated by a tea light candle inside, casting a soft light on the snowy landscape and starry sky.

 1½ hours   Template: see page 109

TOOLS Template, traced • Sheet of glass • Tissue blade • Craft knife • Mixing palette
• Tapestry needle • Pin • Straight-sided drinking glass, approx. 3¼" (8cm) tall
MATERIALS Polymer clay: scraps of gold and white • Liquid polymer clay • Adhesive tape
• Oil paint: white, blue, green • Superglue • Tea light candle

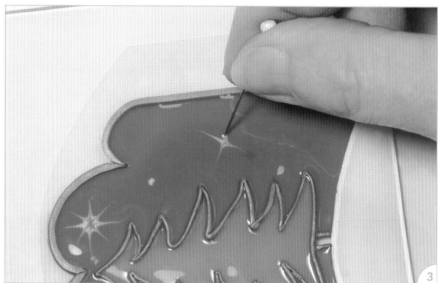

1 Tape the traced template to the underside of the sheet of glass, image side upwards. Form several long threads of white clay, about ¹⁄₃₂" (1mm) thick (see page 18) and press these down along the lines of the snowy hills. Make similar threads of gold clay and use these to outline the trees and the top and sides of the image.

2 Tint some liquid clay with white oil paint (see page 25) and use the needle to scoop up the liquid and apply it, in a thick film, to the hills. Repeat with green for the trees, pushing the liquid into the corners with the point of the needle.

3 To color the sky, apply blue liquid clay. Stud the sky with stars by dropping small pools of white into it and using the pin to drag the edges into points. Bake the piece, on the glass, for 30 minutes.

4 Leave to cool fully, then peel the image off the glass. It should come off easily, but you may need to slide a blade under it to ease it off. Wrap the image round the drinking glass, using a few spots of glue to hold it in place. Place the tea light candle inside the glass. (Never leave a burning candle unattended.)

MORE IDEAS
Design other simple scenes for nightlights. Make light-catchers, to hang at a window, using the same technique.

TIP
Bake the piece as soon as it is finished, or the stars will spread and lose definition.

Translucent grasses lamp

Translucent polymer clay makes beautiful shades for candles, and this striking lamp would be a perfect centerpiece for a dinnertable. When the translucent grasses are lit from within by the candle, they give off a splendid glow.

 1 hour

TOOLS Pasta machine or roller • Wine bottle with straight sides • Craft knife • Cookie sheet (baking sheet) lined with baking parchment
MATERIALS Polymer clay, 2oz (65g) blocks: 2 blocks translucent, scraps of yellow, green, blue and violet • Aluminum foil • Adhesive tape • Jelly jar (jam jar) or tumbler • Tea light candle
MIXTURES To make translucent pastels, tint ½ block of translucent clay with a tiny quantity of each of the colored clays. Do not mix in the colors fully—variegated results look best.

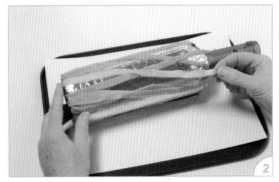

1 Wrap foil around the wine bottle and tape into place. Roll out a sheet of translucent blue clay, about ⅟₁₆" (1.5mm) thick. Use the knife to cut out tapered strips of clay, pointed at one end and about ⅜" (10mm) wide at the other. Vary the length of the strips between about 8" (20cm) and 4" (10cm).

2 Press a strip on the foil-covered bottle, keeping the straight end level with the base of the bottle and allowing the other end to curve upwards at an angle. Repeat with more strips, overlapping them and placing at different angles to give the effect of growing grasses. Roll out the other translucent colors and apply them to the bottle in the same way.

MORE IDEAS
The leaves from the mobile on page 83 could be applied in the same way to make a leafy lamp.

3 Leave some spaces between the grasses for the candlelight to shine through, but avoid large gaps, which will weaken the structure. When the foil is covered all the way around, put the bottle on a cookie sheet (baking sheet) covered in baking parchment. Bake for 30 minutes and leave to cool. Carefully slip the grasses and foil off the bottle, then pull the foil away.

4 Place the candle inside the jar or tumbler, and slide it into the lamp. This will prevent the flame from coming into contact with the clay and makes the lamp much safer. (However, never leave a burning candle unattended.)

TIP
Do not overbake translucent clay— it is more likely to discolor than other colors.

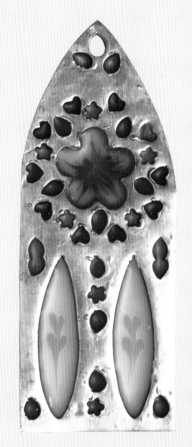

Stained-glass window decoration (page 105)

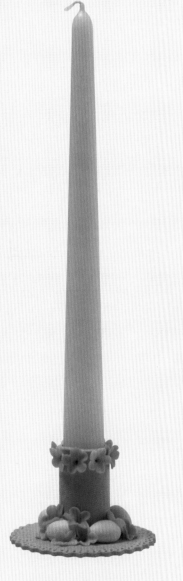

Easter candlestick (page 100)

Pumpkin lantern (page 103)

CHAPTER 7
Celebrations

Top: Snowman (page 104)
Bottom: Party bag clip (page 98)

Cards

Iris window card

To make translucent transfers with liquid polymer clay, images from color magazines and catalogs can be used. A stained-glass motif provides the image for this stylish card, mounted on acetate so that light can shine through it.

 45 minutes

TOOLS Paintbrush • Set square • Heavy-duty craft knife • Metal ruler
MATERIALS Liquid polymer clay • Picture, measuring approx. 1½″ x 2¼″ (4cm x 6cm), cut out of a color magazine or catalog—leave a border, ¼″ (6 mm) wide, all around the image • Stiff card in a color to match the picture: 8½″ x 6″ (22cm x 15cm) • White paper: 4¼″ x 6″ (11cm x 15cm) • Acetate sheet: 3½″ x 4½″ (9cm x 12cm) • PVA glue • Black pen

1 Paint a thin sheet of liquid clay over the image. Bake for 20 minutes at 300°F (150°C) or the temperature recommended by the manufacturer. Drop into a glass of water and leave until the paper is soaked through.

2 Rub the soaked paper off the back of the image to reveal the translucent transfer. If the image is fragile, it has not been baked at a sufficiently high temperature. Trim the image neatly. Score the card and fold it in half. Using the set square, ruler and craft knife, cut out a window in the center front. This should be large enough to give a border of ⅜″ (1cm) around the picture.

MORE IDEAS
This simple technique can be used to make a wonderful selection of "stained-glass" cards. Try using handmade papers, perhaps inset with pressed flowers, for the card.

3 Glue the acetate to the inside of the window and the white paper to the inside back of the card. Glue the transfer to the center of the acetate window. With the black pen, draw a decorative line around the acetate window to complete it.

> ### TIP
> *The liquid clay should be painted onto the image as thinly as possible, but make sure that the entire image is covered by a thin film, or there will be holes in the transfer.*

Lacy valentine card

Handmade valentine cards are always appreciated, and are the perfect way to say "I love you" to someone special. This pretty card uses lace impressions and pearlescent powders to create a really sumptuous card with an antique feel.

 45 minutes

Template: see page 110

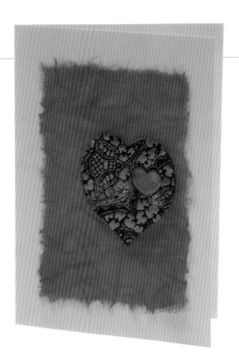

TOOLS Pasta machine or roller • Ceramic tile • Template, traced and cut out • Heart cutter: ½" (13mm) • Fine paintbrush • Scrap(s) of lace
MATERIALS Polymer clay, 2oz (65g) blocks: ¼ block black • Pearlescent powders: gold, and copper or metallic red • Red mulberry paper (or any decorative paper): 6" x 8" (15cm x 20cm) • Water • Cream card: 8½" x 6" (22cm x 15cm) • PVA glue

1 Roll the black clay into a sheet, ¹⁄₁₆" (1.5mm) thick, on the tile. Lay a piece of lace over the sheet and roll over it firmly with the roller. Reposition the lace and roll again. Repeat until the clay is covered with impressions. Use the template to cut out the heart shape. Dip your finger in gold powder and brush it over the clay to highlight the design.

2 Cut a small heart out of the large one with the heart cutter and remove the piece. Roll out a small sheet of black, the same thickness as before, and brush with copper powder. Cut a small heart from this and press it into the gap in the large heart. Bake on the tile for 20 minutes.

3 Score the center of the cream card and fold it in half. With a pencil, lightly mark a rectangle on the mulberry paper, 4¼" x 3" (11cm x 7.5cm). Draw a line just inside the pencil lines with a wet brush. Tear the paper along the line, giving a neat torn edge. Glue the rectangle to the center of the card and glue the heart on it, offset center right.

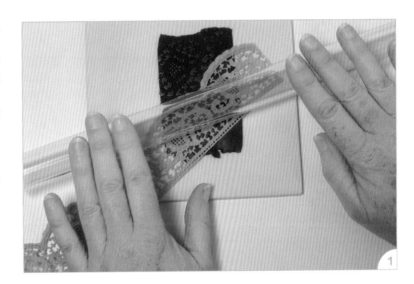

MORE IDEAS
Make a pearly heart using white clay and pearlescent powder, and complement it with a pastel mulberry paper.

TIP
The clay will be stuck firmly to the tile after the lace has been impressed into it, but will come off easily after baking.

Playful children card

This cheery card, showing two little girls playing in the sunshine, would be ideal for a child's birthday. Their dresses feature a symmetrical pattern that results from an intriguing technique involving cutting into lightly marbled clay.

 45 minutes

TOOLS Craft knife • Ceramic tile • Pasta machine or roller • Circle cutter: ½" (13mm) • Tapestry needle
MATERIALS Polymer clay: Small amounts of yellow, blue, crimson, flesh, brown, black, gold • Green card: 8½" x 3½" (22cm x 9cm), scored and folded in half • Black pen • PVA glue

1 Press together small pieces of yellow, blue and crimson clays to make a ½" (13mm) ball. Marble the mixture lightly (see page 24) and form it into a rectangular shape, about ¼" (6mm) thick. Stand the rectangle upright on its long edge and slice down the center lengthways. Open out the two halves to reveal a symmetrical pattern. Press these together side by side on the tile. Make a second split rectangle.

2 To make the girls' dresses, trim each rectangle to make a triangle ¾" (20mm) high. For the limbs, take a log of flesh clay, 1/12" (2mm) thick. Cut four ⅜" (10mm) lengths. For the arms, point both ends of two lengths and press on the shoulders. Apply two ⅛" (3mm) balls of crimson clay to the bottom of the legs to make shoes and press the legs on below the skirt. For the head, apply a 3/16" (5mm) ball of flesh.

3 To make hair, curl a very thin thread of gold clay over the head. Poke holes for eyes and mouth. Make a second girl with blue shoes and brown hair. To make the sun, cut a circle from a sheet of yellow, 1/16" (1.5mm) thick, and cut thin strips for the rays. Bake all the pieces for 20 minutes and when cool, glue to the card using the photographs as a guide. Mark a line of black ink underneath the girls' feet for the ground.

MORE IDEAS

Boys can be made in the same way as girls, but cut the patterned rectangle into the shape of overalls. For the arms, make sleeves from colored clay and add tiny balls of flesh for the hands.

TIP
If you do not like the pattern when you cut open the marbled rectangle, simply marble the clay together and cut open again.

Rose topiary card

A dainty rosebush in a terracotta pot decorates this pretty card. The technique used mimics the ancient decorative craft of paper quilling, where strips of colored paper are coiled and glued down to make a design. The polymer clay version is quick and easy to do.

 1 hour

TOOLS Pasta machine or roller • Tissue blade • Craft knife • Tapestry needle • Small teardrop cutter: ³⁄₁₆" (5mm) • Ceramic tile • Pinking shears or decorative scissors
MATERIALS Polymer clay: small amounts of pink, white, leaf green, dark brown and copper • White lace paper (or any pretty decorative paper): 2¾" x 4¼" (7cm x 11cm) • Cream card, scored and folded in half: 8½" x 6" (22cm x 15cm) • PVA glue
MIXTURES To make pale pink: ⅜" (10mm) ball of white, ⅜" (10mm) ball of pink

1 To make the pale pink roses, roll out the pale pink clay into a sheet about ¹⁄₃₂" (1mm) thick. Use the blade to cut several strips, ¹⁄₁₆" (1.5mm) wide. Place the knife blade against the side of a strip and roll it up with the needle until it is about ¼" (6mm) in diameter. Make ten roses. Repeat the process with pink clay to make seven more roses.

2 Press the roses on the tile in the pattern shown. Roll out a sheet of leaf green clay, ¹⁄₃₂" (1mm) thick, and cut out 20 leaves with the cutter. Press pairs of leaves around the outside of the roses, marking veins. Press the remaining four pale pink roses on the tile and apply a pair of leaves by each one, marking veins as before.

3 Cut a strip of dark brown clay for the trunk, ¾" (20mm) long and ¹⁄₃₂" (1mm) thick. Roll out a sheet of copper clay, ¹⁄₃₂" (1mm) thick, and cut out a flowerpot, ⅝" (17mm) tall. Decorate it with two twisted strips of copper clay. Bake all the pieces on the tile for 20 minutes and remove when cool. Glue the lace paper to the card, then glue the rosebush on top. Glue the single roses in the corners.

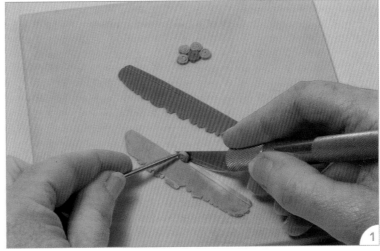

VARIATION
The rosebush can flower in any color you like—lemon and deep yellow clays look especially good glued to lace paper on a pale blue card.

> **TIP**
> *It is essential to use firm or well-leached (see page 17) clay for this project, or the rolled roses will be difficult to make.*

Toucan card

A toucan surveys the scene in a tropical jungle—brilliant colors and a bold design make this a particularly cheerful card.

 30 minutes

TOOLS Ceramic tile • Tapestry needle • Craft knife • Pointed tool
MATERIALS Polymer clay, 2oz (65g) blocks: ¼ block black, scraps of white, crimson, yellow, blue and gray • Blank card: sky blue with window aperture 3" (8cm) square • Bright yellow card, 4" x 4" (10cm x 10cm) • Artist's pastels: brown, light green, dark green, crimson • Fixative for pastels (hairspray works well) • PVA glue

1 To make the toucan's body, form a ½" (13mm) ball of black clay into an oval. Press this down on the tile. Make the breast by shaping a ¼" (6mm) ball of white clay into an oval, and flatten it slightly. Press it on the left side of the body. For the curved bill, make logs of crimson, black and yellow clay, ⅛" (3mm) thick. Roll these into a striped, tapered log, pointed at one end. Trim to 1" (25mm) long. Press on the body, above the white breast.

2 Make the eye surround from a ⅛" (3mm) ball of pale blue clay, and press on to the head. Pierce the center and insert a small black ball for the eye. For the tail feathers, flatten a log of black clay, cut slices and apply them to the bottom of the body. For the wing, shape a ⅜" (10mm) ball of black into a teardrop, flatten it and press on to the body. Mark feathers with the eye of the needle.

3 Make the foot from a small teardrop of gray. Bake the toucan on the tile for 30 minutes. Glue the yellow card inside the card aperture and sketch a leafy branch on it with pastels. Spray the pastels with fixative. Glue the toucan to the branch.

> **TIP**
> *Keep the body and wing pieces fairly thin so that the card will fit into an envelope.*

Stamped card

Stamps featuring Native American petroglyph images have been used to make this highly unusual card, which is suitable for any occasion. When choosing stamps, select those that have well-defined images.

 30 minutes

TOOLS Ceramic tile • Pasta machine or roller • Tissue blade • 3 petroglyph stamps with an image approximately 1" (25mm) square, or any square stamp

MATERIALS Polymer clay, 2oz (65g) blocks: ¼ block beige, ¼ block dark brown • Talcum powder • Pearlescent powder: gold • Stamp pads: pink and blue • Blank card, apricot: 5½" (14cm) square • Brown mulberry paper, torn into a 4" (10cm) square (see page 93) • PVA glue

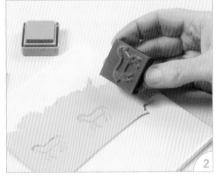

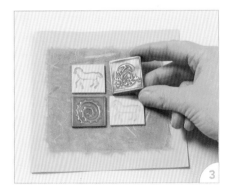

1 Roll out a sheet of brown clay, ¹⁄₁₆" (1.5mm) thick, on the ceramic tile. Dust with talcum powder and use two of the stamps to make two tiles, 1" (25mm) square. Stamp firmly and cut around the tiles with the blade. Brush gold powder over the surface with your finger.

2 Roll out the beige clay on the ceramic tile in the same way. Lightly ink the second stamp and stamp it into the clay. Cut out two tiles, 1" (25mm) square, as in Step 1. Bake all the tiles on the ceramic tile for 30 minutes.

3 Glue the mulberry paper to the center of the card. Glue on the polymer clay tiles, arranged in a square with a space between them, and alternating the light and dark tiles.

MORE IDEAS
Oriental stamps make stylish images—try stamping terracotta clay with a Chinese character, then brush with gold powder. A butterfly makes a simple, airy motif— try stamping with brown ink into pearl white clay.

TIP
To tear paper in a straight line, draw a wet paintbrush along a pencilled guideline. The paper will part easily where it is wet (see page 93).

Parties

Party bag clip

This bright clip makes a snappy seal for a child's party bag full of goodies. Clips are versatile little helpers—use them to hold papers together, clamp rubber boots in pairs or, with a small magnet glued to the back, to clip notes to the fridge.

 30 minutes

TOOLS Pasta machine or roller • Tissue blade • Ceramic tile • Paintbrush
MATERIALS Polymer clay, 2oz (65g) blocks: ¼ block crimson, ¼ block yellow, ¼ block blue • Spring-loaded wooden clothes pin • Acrylic paint: yellow • Superglue

1 Form a log of crimson clay, ⅛" (3mm) thick and about 6" (15cm) long. Cut it into four lengths. Repeat with the yellow clay. Press the lengths together side by side, alternating the colors. Roll them out on the tile in the direction of the stripes until they form a striped sheet, about ¹⁄₁₆" (1.5mm) thick.

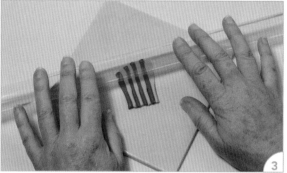

2 To make the parcel, trim the edges diagonally across the stripes to make a 1¼" (30mm) square. For the ribbon, roll out a sheet of blue clay, ¹⁄₃₂" (1mm) thick, and cut out a long strip, ³⁄₁₆" (5mm) wide. Apply lengths of this in a cross, trimming the ends to fit.

3 To make the trailing ends of the bow, cut two ¾" (20mm) lengths from the same blue strip, and notch a "V" in one end of each. Press on top of the crossed ribbons. To make the bow, cut a 2" (5cm) length, fold the ends into the center and wrap with another short length. Press on top of the trailing ends. Bake the parcel on the tile for 20 minutes. Paint the pin yellow and glue the parcel to the center of one side.

MORE IDEAS
These little clips just ask to be made in a rainbow of colors! Paint the pins to match the parcels. The position of the bow can also be altered.

> **TIP**
> *If you find it hard to cut the square freehand, make a small card template and cut round that.*

Balloon place marker

Make young party guests feel special with these delightful balloon place markers. Colored wire, in a variety of colors and gauges, is available from craft or jewelry materials stores.

 30 minutes

TOOLS Craft knife • Wire cutters • Ceramic tile • Pen with a smooth, round barrel
MATERIALS Polymer clay, 65g (2oz) blocks: ½ block blue, scraps of crimson and yellow • Red metallic wire (18 gauge): 6½" (17cm) long • Superglue • Small card for the child's name

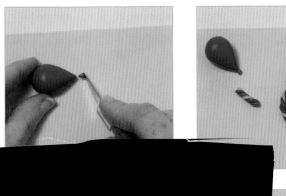

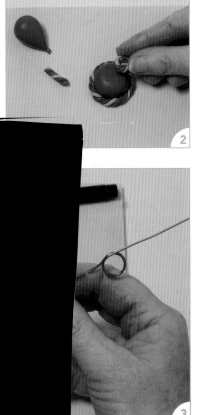

1 To make the balloon, form a ¾" (20mm) ball of blue clay, and roll it gently between your palms to point one end into a balloon shape. Form a ¹⁄₁₆" (1.5mm) ball of blue into a tiny cone, and press it on the lower end of the balloon.

2 Make the base from a 1" (25mm) ball of blue and press on the tile. Make logs from each of the blue, crimson and yellow clays, ¹⁄₁₂" (2mm) thick and 6" (15cm) long, and twist together into   rope. Wrap it around the base and t so that the ends butt neatly. With th rope, make a small ring and press o base.

3 Wrap the middle of the length of pen barrel twice, so that the two en opposite directions from the coil. M the center of the base to take the w Push one end of the wire into the c of the balloon. Bake the pieces for When cool, glue the other end of t base and slip the card into the wir

MORE IDEAS
As with the party bag clip, place n
could be made in a sizzling variety
for a really stunning party table. (
be coordinated to match the table
and decorations.

le as possible so that

Easter

Easter candlestick

Delicate pastel flowers and eggs decorate this pretty woven candleholder, which will look elegant as a table centerpiece. Take care not to let the candle burn right down to the holder or the clay will burn. (Never leave burning candles unattended.)

 1 hour

TOOLS Ceramic tile • Craft knife • Pasta machine or roller • Pointed tool • Flower cutter: ½" (13mm) • Leaf cutter: ¾" (20mm)

MATERIALS Polymer clay, 2oz (65g) blocks: 1 block ochre, ¼ block white, ¼ block translucent, small quantities of leaf green, crimson and yellow • White candle • Aluminum foil • Talcum powder

MIXTURES To make pastel green, pastel pink and pastel yellow: divide the translucent clay into three and mix a little leaf green into one, crimson into another and yellow into the third

1 To make the base, form some of the ochre clay into a log, ⅛" (3mm) thick and about 12" (30cm) long. Fold it in half and twist into a rope. Start in the center of the tile and coil the rope into a spiral mat, adding more ropes as necessary, until it measures 3½" (9cm) in diameter. Press each new rope against the previous one to secure and finish the end neatly.

2 Wrap the base of the candle in foil and hold it upright on the center of the spiral mat. To make the candleholder, form a twisted rope of ochre clay and wind it around the base of the candle, adding more lengths as necessary, until the sides are 1¼" (3cm) high.

3 Roll out the pastel clays to about 1/16" (1.5mm) thick, dust with talcum powder, and cut flowers and leaves. Make a hole in the center of each flower and and mark veins on the leaves. Press on the base. Form eggs from ⅜" (10mm) balls of white clay, and tuck them in amongst the flowers. Remove the candle and bake the candleholder on the tile for 30 minutes.

MORE IDEAS
The lacy holder in the photograph is made in the same way but uses sheets of beige clay, cut to size, instead of the coiled ropes. The base is cut out with a fluted cutter and decorated by pricking a lace design with a tapestry needle.

TIP
Use firm clay to make coiling easier. If the clay is too soft, leach it for a few hours (see page 17).

Easter bunny

This adorable little brown rabbit would look perfect sitting in a bowl of mini chocolate Easter eggs. Polymer clay is ideal for modelling the rounded shapes of small animals.

🕐 30 minutes

TOOLS • Ceramic tile • Craft knife • Pointed tool • Small paintbrush with a smooth, round handle

MATERIALS Polymer clay, 2oz (65g) blocks: ¼ block brown, small pieces of white, pink and black

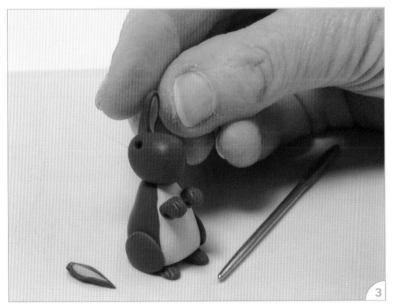

1 To make the body, form a ¾" (20mm) ball of brown clay, shape into a cone and press on the tile. For the chest, apply a thin sheet of white clay to one side and smooth the joins. To make the head, form a ½" (13mm) ball of brown into an oval. For the paws, form a log of brown, ³⁄₁₆" (5mm) thick, and cut four ¼" (6mm) lengths. Shape these into ovals.

2 For the back paws, press two of the ovals on the tile, a little apart. Press the body on top, leaving the paws to protrude slightly. For the front paws, press the other two ovals on the body, bending the tops over. Mark claws with the knife. For the haunches, flatten two ¼" (6mm) balls of brown, and press on the sides of the body.

3 Ears: form two ³⁄₁₆" (5mm) balls of brown into tapered logs ½" (13mm) long. Make the inner ear from a smaller log of pink and shape it with the handle of the paintbrush. Make two holes on top of the head and insert the ears. Poke holes for eye sockets and insert small black balls for the eyes. Apply a tiny pink ball for the nose and a ³⁄₁₆" (5mm) ball of white for the tail. Bake the rabbit for 30 minutes.

MORE IDEAS
Make lots of friends and relations for this rabbit in different sizes and colors—white and gray look equally charming.

TIP
To prevent the rabbit's ears from flopping down during baking, make a little collar of paper and slip it over the ears.

Halloween

Ghost fridge magnets

These spooky characters are made in glow-in-the-dark polymer clay. They take very little time to make and will give a lively Halloween look to your fridge. The clay glows in the dark after exposure to a bright light.

 30 minutes

TOOLS Ceramic tile • Craft knife
MATERIALS Polymer clay, 2oz (65g) blocks: 1 block glow-in-the-dark clay (makes lots of ghosts), scraps of black • Small magnets
• Superglue

1 Form some glow-in-the-dark clay into a " (25mm) ball. Shape this into a tapered log, 2¼" (7cm) long, and flatten the middle of it. Pinch out the clay into arms on either side of the body.

2 Flatten the ends of the arms to make the hands. Make three cuts in each for the fingers and splay them out. Pinch the top of the head into a point and give the bottom of the ghost a slight "S" shape.

3 For the eyes, form two small ¹⁄₁₆" (1.5mm) balls of black clay, and shape into ovals. Press on the head. Bake the ghost on the tile for about 30 minutes. When it is cool, glue the magnet to the back.

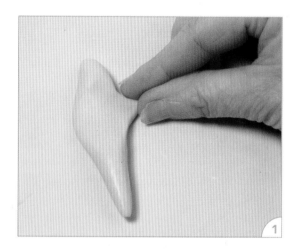

MORE IDEAS
Follow these instructions to make ghosts of all sizes. Instead of a magnet, you could glue a pin or brooch back on the back to turn the ghosts into scary Halloween brooches.

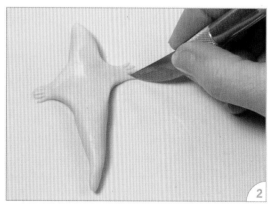

TIP
Make sure that your hands are really clean before handling glow-in-the-dark clay, because it marks easily.

Pumpkin lantern

Add a special touch of magic to your Halloween décor with this mini pumpkin lantern. The features are made from an infill of liquid polymer clay, and glow wickedly in the candle flame.

 30 minutes

Template: see page 110

TOOLS Pasta machine or roller • 2 ceramic tiles • Template, traced and cut out • Craft knife • Thick tapestry needle • Set square
MATERIALS Polymer clay, 2oz (65g) blocks: 1 block translucent, ⅛ block orange, ¼ block copper, scraps of black • Liquid polymer clay • Superglue • Baby food jar • Tea light candle
MIXTUREs To make translucent orange: combine the translucent and orange clays

1 Roll the translucent orange clay into a sheet, ⅛" (3mm) thick, and place it on the tile. Use the template to cut out the pumpkin shape and the facial features. Score the lines of the design on the pumpkin with the needle. Form a small, tapered log for the stalk and press it on top of the pumpkin.

2 Form threads of black clay, 1⁄32" (1mm) thick (see page 22) and apply these to the pumpkin to follow the scored lines of the spider's web.

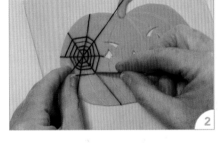

3 Make a tiny spider by pressing down eight short lengths of thread for the legs and then applying a ball of black for the body. Fill the cut out features with a generous layer of liquid polymer clay.

4 Roll out a sheet of copper clay, ⅛" (3mm) thick, on the second tile and cut a 2¼" (6cm) square. Bake the pumpkin and square on their tiles for 30 minutes. Glue the pumpkin to the square, using a set square to make sure it is vertical. Place the candle in the baby food jar and set it on the copper square. (Never leave a burning candle unattended.)

> **TIP**
> *When the pumpkin is baked, it can be removed from the tile more easily by gently sliding a blade between the baked clay and the tile.*

Christmas

Snowman

This well-dressed snowman looks delightful decorating a mantelpiece. If you make him some friends, you can have a whole gang of snowmen congregating on a windowsill to make an amusing Chrismas scene.

 30 minutes

TOOLS Ceramic tile • Craft knife • Pointed tool • Tapestry needle • Pasta machine or roller
MATERIALS Polymer clay, 2oz (65g) blocks: ¼ block white, scraps of orange, red and black

1 To make the body, form a 1" (25mm) ball of white clay into a slightly tapered shape. For the head, press a ⅝" (15mm) ball of white on the body. To make arms, roll a log, ³⁄₁₆" (5mm) thick, and cut two lengths of ⅜" (10mm). Form each into a tapered log, and press on the body in a curve.

2 For buttons, appliqué thin slices from a thin black log on the snowman's front (see page 25). To make the hat brim, flatten a ¼" (6mm) ball of black clay and press it on the head. For the crown of the hat, cut a ¼" (6mm) length from a log of black, ¼" (6mm) thick. Press it on the brim.

3 Make holes for the eyes and press a ¹⁄₁₆" (1.5mm) ball of black into each hole. Add a small cone of orange for the nose and mark a smiling mouth. To make the scarf, roll out a sheet of red clay, ¹⁄₃₂" (1mm) thick, and cut two strips, ³⁄₁₆" (5mm) wide and 1" (25mm) long. Cut a fringe on one end of each. Wrap a third strip around the neck and arrange the fringed pieces of the scarf. Bake the snowman for 30 minutes.

MORE IDEAS

To make striped scarves for the snowman, use the method for making striped sheets of clay on page 98. You could make a broom from a log of brown clay with thin strips of ochre clay applied around one end, bake it and then press it on the snowman before baking him.

TIP
To make a row of snowmen quickly, create a mini production line— make a row of bodies, then press on all the heads, and so on.

Stained-glass window decoration

The glorious stained-glass windows of medieval cathedrals inspired this colorful polymer clay decoration. Despite its apparent intricacy, it is quick and easy to make. Display it in a window, so that the light can shine through the "glass" panels, or use it to decorate the Christmas tree.

 30 minutes   Template: see page 110

TOOLS Ceramic tile • Flower cutters: ½" (13mm) and ³⁄₁₆" (5mm) • Heart cutter: ³⁄₁₆" (5mm) • Teardrop cutter: ³⁄₁₆" (5mm) • Leaf cutter: 1½" (4cm) long • Large tapestry needle • Palette for mixing • Darning needle • Template, traced and cut out
MATERIALS Polymer clay, 2oz (65g) blocks: 1 block black • Liquid polymer clay • Oil paints: magenta, yellow, blue, green • Gold cord

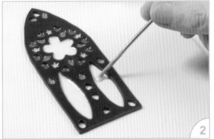

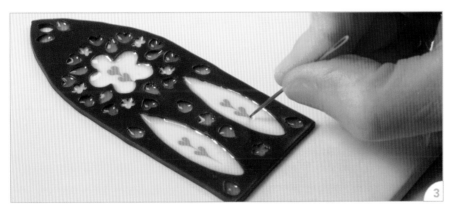

MORE IDEAS
Make and bake a silver window in the same way. To give the effect of antique silver, apply silver burnishing paste. For an ethereal effect, use pearl white clay instead of black and tint the liquid clay with cool, pastel colors.

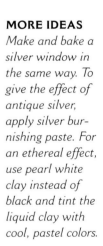

1 Roll the black clay into a sheet, ¹⁄₁₆" (1.5mm) thick, and place it on the tile. Use the template to cut out the window. Cut out the design with the cutters, using the template as a guide.

2 Tint the liquid clay with the oil paints to make four different colors (see page 25). Use the tapestry needle to apply the liquid, in a thick layer, to the cut-out areas. In each large window, apply two drops of magenta in the center of the yellow background. Draw the tip of the needle through the two drops, from top to bottom, to make the hearts.

3 Bake the window, on the tile, for 30 minutes. When the tile is cool, carefully slice under the window with a blade to remove it from the tile. Tie a gold cord through the hole at the top for hanging.

> **TIP**
> *If you enjoy using liquid clay, save your mixed colors in small jars to use again (it keeps well).*

Templates

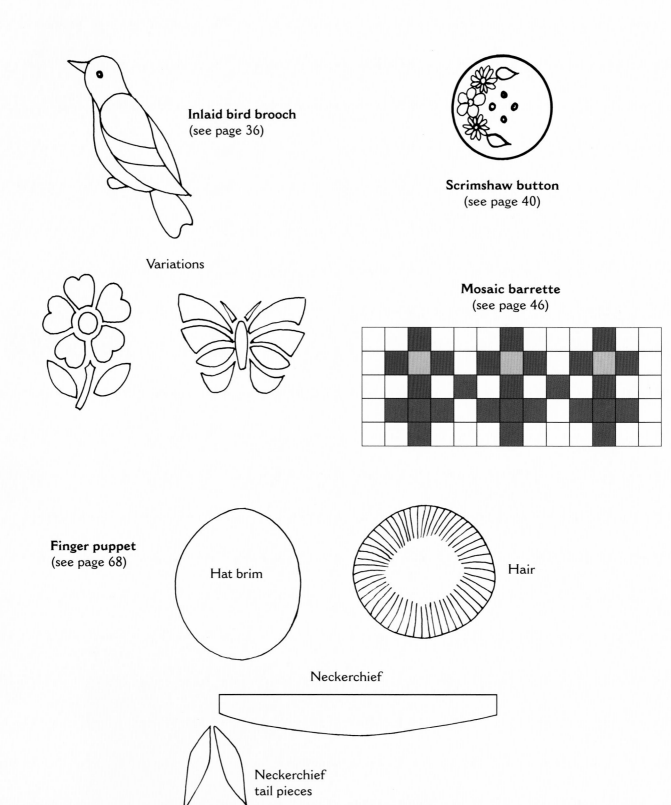

Inlaid bird brooch
(see page 36)

Scrimshaw button
(see page 40)

Variations

Mosaic barrette
(see page 46)

Finger puppet
(see page 68)

Hat brim

Hair

Neckerchief

Neckerchief
tail pieces

Owl jumping jack
(see page 69)

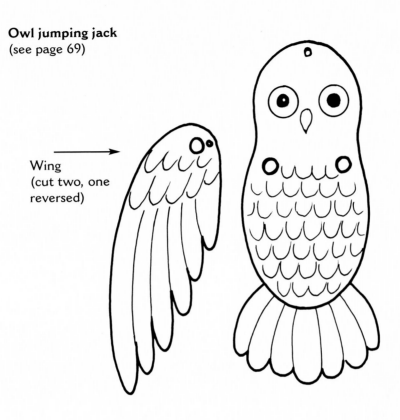

Wing
(cut two, one
reversed)

Pocket doll
(see page 70)

Bodice

Skirt

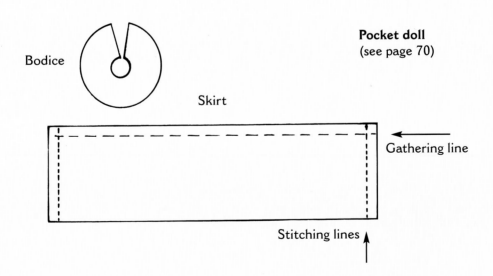

Gathering line

Stitching lines

House
(see page 73)

Roof (cut two)

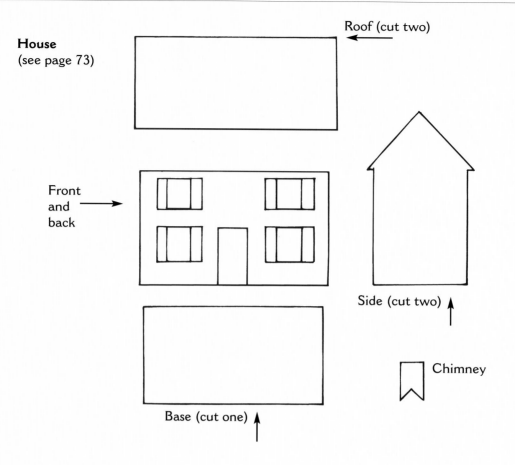

Front
and
back

Side (cut two)

Chimney

Base (cut one)

Leaf mobile
(see page 83)

Faux wood picture frame
(see page 85)

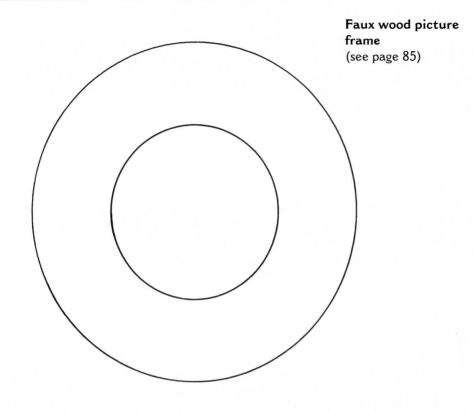

Snowscene nightlight
(see page 88)

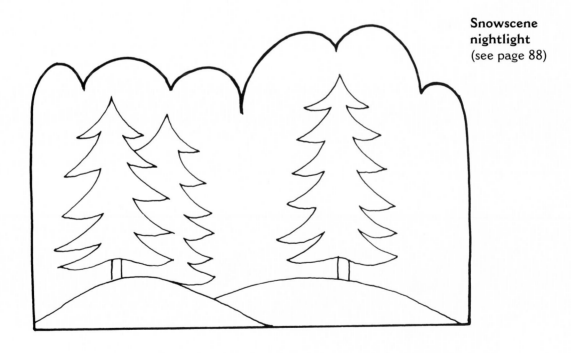

Lacy valentine card
(see page 93)

**Stained-glass
window decoration**
(see page 105)

Pumpkin lantern
(see page 103)

  TEMPLATES

Index

Suppliers

Polymer clays are widely available in craft and art material stores, and also by mail order from craft suppliers. If you have problems finding the clays, the following suppliers should be able to help.

AUSTRALIA

Rossdale Pty Ltd
351–353 Warrigal Road
Cheltenham 3192
Victoria
Tel: 001 613 9583 4411
E-mail: sales@rossdale.com.au
(Premo, Sculpey)

Staedtler (Pacific) Pty Ltd
PO Box 576, 1 Inman Road
Dee Why, NSW 2099
Tel: 0061 2 9982 4555
(Fimo)

CANADA

KJP Crafts
PO Box 5009 Merivale Depot
Nepean, Ontario K2C 3H3
Tel: 613 225 6926
E-mail: kjpcrafts@attcanada.net
Website: www.kjpcrafts.com
(Premo, Sculpey)

Staedtler Mars Ltd
5725 McLaughlin Road
Mississauga, ON L5R 3K5
Tel : 001 905 501 9008
(Fimo)

NEW ZEALAND

Zigzag Polymer Clay Supplies Ltd
8 Cherry Place, Casebrook
Christchurch 8005
New Zealand
Tel: (+64) 3 359 2989
E-mail: sales@zigzag.co.nz
Website: www.polymerclay.co.nz
www.zigzag.co.nz
(Polymer clays, tools etc.)

UNITED KINGDOM

The Polymer Clay Pit
3 Harts Lane, Wortham
Diss, Norfolk IP22 1PQ
Tel/fax: 01379 890176
E-mail: info@polymerclaypit.co.uk
Website: www.polymerclaypit.co.uk
(Polymer clays, tools etc.)

UNITED STATES
Clay Factory of Escondido
PO Box 460598
Escondido, CA 92046~0598

Tel: 1 877 728 5739
E-mail:
clayfactoryinc@clayfactoryinc.com
Website: www.clayfactoryinc.com
(Premo, Cernit, tools etc.)

American Art Clay Co. Inc.
4717 W. Sixteenth St.
Indianapolis, IN 46222
Tel: 001 317 244 6871
(Fimo)

POLYMER CLAY ORGANIZATIONS
Please send a stamped addressed envelope when enquiring about membership.

The British Polymer Clay Guild
48 Park Close
Hethersett, Norwich NR9 3EW
United Kingdom

The National Polymer Clay Guild
PMB 345
1350 Beverly Road, 115
McLean VA 22 1 01
USA

WEBSITE
Current information on suppliers and organizations can be found at:
http://www.polymerclaypit.co.uk

Acknowledgments

I would like to thank Juliette and Sally at The Polymer Clay Pit for their help, friendship and tea-making while this book was being written. Thanks also to Marionette and her crew; and to Maureen, Peter and Cobbold's Tales... for all the much-needed stress relief!